FIRM FOUNDATIONS

FIRM FOUNDATIONS

Daily Readings from
Great Chapters of the Bible

PETER JEFFERY
and
OWEN MILTON

EVANGELICAL PRESS OF WALES

© Evangelical Press of Wales, 1981
First published 1981
Second edition 1987
Reprinted 1993

ISBN 1 85049 031 7
(First edition – ISBN 0 900898 62 3)

Cover design:
Rhiain M. Davies (Cain)

Cover picture:
Mumbles Head, near Swansea
(by courtesy of the Wales Tourist Board)

Published by the Evangelical Press of Wales
Bryntirion, Bridgend, Mid Glamorgan CF31 4DX
Printed in Wales by D. Brown & Sons Ltd., Bridgend

Contents

Introduction

THE purpose of this book is to provide a two-month Bible reading course for those beginning the Christian life. The chapters dealt with have been chosen because they are among the most well-known and best loved in the Bible. No attempt is made here to give a detailed exposition; that would be impossible in the space allowed. The intention rather is to introduce you to these great chapters, and to draw from them some of the basic truths and lessons which you need to learn early in your Christian life.

On some pages you will find quotations from Christian books. These will throw further light on the passages you are reading and will also make you aware of godly writers whose books can be of help to you throughout your Christian life.

The comments are based on the text of the New International Version of the Bible.

*   *   *

One of the marks that you are a Christian is that you have a desire to read and understand the Bible. Probably before your conversion the Bible was a closed book to you, looked upon as something rather ancient and not relevant to your life. You have already realized that this is far from the truth. 'Like newborn babies, crave pure spiritual milk, so that by it you may grow up in your salvation' (1 Peter 2:2). When you were born physically you needed and wanted milk; it kept you alive and enabled you to grow. You have now been born spiritually, and inevitably there will be a craving for spiritual milk. This you get only from the Word of God, so you must come to the Bible every day. What profit you receive from the Bible will depend to a large extent on how you approach it.

7

Firstly, *learn to love the Bible*. It is a unique book, quite unlike any other publication. This is not the word of man: 'Above all, you must understand that no prophecy of Scripture came about by the prophet's own interpretation. For prophecy never had its origin in the will of man, but men spoke from God as they were carried along by the Holy Spirit' (2 Peter 1:20,21). The Bible does not merely contain the Word of God, it *is* the Word of God – all of it. It is a most precious gift, and has been given to us by our heavenly Father as our absolute authority. As well as being the unique source of information about God, it is also an inspiration, an encouragement, sometimes a rebuke, but always a guide. As a Christian you cannot do without the Bible.

Did you know that men of God gave their lives so that we could have the Bible in our own language? We would urge you to read the story of William Tyndale in the book *God's Outlaw* by Brian Edwards (Evangelical Press).

Secondly, *come to the Scriptures prayerfully*, seeking the illumination of the Holy Spirit without whose help you will never understand the truths that God would have us believe. Come wanting to learn and eager to obey all that the Bible teaches. If you approach the Word of God in this way you will discover a rich treasure-house that will be a blessing to you every day of your life. Turn for a moment to Psalm 119. Almost every verse in this long psalm makes reference to Scripture, and we would especially point you to verses 9-16, 18, 24 and 133.

Thirdly, when you start reading the Bible, *do not start in Genesis*. It is good to read first of all about Jesus in one of the Gospels, but even then you need help and teaching. This is why Bible reading notes can be invaluable. A good place to start is in Mark's Gospel, using the notes by John Blanchard entitled *Read, Mark, Learn* (Evangelical Press). The reason we have written our notes is because we believe that early in a Christian's spiritual life he needs to be introduced briefly to a cross-section of the great passages of the Bible.

The way to benefit from Bible reading notes is to use them in the morning, if possible, and

a. Pray for understanding.

b. Read the set daily chapter carefully.

c. Read the notes and look up every Bible reference given, whether in the passage already read or elsewhere.

d. Consider quietly the lessons learnt and throughout the day let your mind go back to these truths when you have a spare moment.

New Life

THIS chapter speaks of two important elements in Christian experience—rebirth or regeneration, and faith. They occur in that order in the chapter and in the experience of every individual.

Regeneration

The path to heaven begins when a person is 'born again'. Before this he is, in the words of Paul, 'dead in transgressions and sins'. This explains why he cannot 'see' or 'enter' the kingdom of God. He is as incapable of moving toward heaven as a corpse is of turning itself in any direction. A force from outside is necessary. Being born again is the work of the Holy Spirit in us, stirring us, raising us and giving us power. It is the planting of life in that which was dead.

So far, the sinner contributes nothing to what is happening to him. The work is entirely God's. But the work does not end there. For now Jesus speaks of believing, and later in the chapter we find John the Baptist doing so. It is not the Holy Spirit who must believe—it is the sinner. And this he is able to do only *after* he has been born again.

Faith

But what must he believe? The question is better asked, In whom must he believe? For faith is not merely a matter of believing certain facts, although that is included, but rather trust and wholehearted commitment to a Person, the Lord Jesus Christ. The facts are that God gave His Son to die on a cross for the sins of men and women. Faith is our total personal response to God's Son. By this means we are rescued from the condemnation and wrath of God.

Although these two features are closely associated in the

11

Bible, they are both clearly distinguished. In your own experience you will not be able to separate them. No one can say, 'I was born again then', and later, 'I believed then'. They serve, however, to show our absolute dependence on God, and the necessity for us to believe. Bearing this in mind will make sure that we do not become lop-sided in our understanding of the gospel.

> *When Jesus speaks about entering the kingdom of God, it is clear that the expression is equivalent to 'having everlasting life' or being saved. The kingdom of God is the realm in which His rule is recognized and obeyed and in which His grace prevails. Before one can see that kingdom, before one can have everlasting life in any sense, one must be born from above. It is very clear, therefore, that there is an act of God which precedes any act of man.*
>
> William Hendriksen

NOTES

The Man Born Blind

A problem (verse 2)

What a very odd question! That the man's parents might have been responsible for his blindness we can appreciate. But how could the man have brought his blindness upon himself if he was *born* blind? Had he been guilty of sin while still in his mother's womb? For the disciples this man was clearly a mere topic for discussion and no more. Jesus refuses to be drawn into a debate. Here He gives the disciples a brief answer, but swiftly pinpoints a more important matter. Remember there are some questions that Jesus declines to answer, not because He cannot, but because of the spirit in which they are asked. (See Matthew 21:23-27; Luke 13:23-30.) We must beware of unprofitable discussions and idle curiosity.

Jesus sees the man and his plight as a means of glorifying God. Notice the difference in approach. The disciples ask, 'How did he come to be like this?' Jesus asks, 'What can we do for him?' It is obvious which is the more worthy question.

A miracle (verses 6,7)

John's accounts of the miracles of Jesus refer to them as signs. The giving of sight to the blind man and the removing of his darkness is a sign pointing to the claim of verse 5—'I am the light of the world'.

Our Lord could have given the man his sight by speaking a word. There was no healing property in the mud or in the pool. The various ways in which Jesus performed His miracles show us that He is not limited to a particular means. The name of the pool (Siloam) and its interpretation ('Sent') remind us of a deeper truth. Christ is God's Sent One. He is our Siloam. In Him we may wash away our sins and receive spiritual sight.

A controversy (verses 9-34)

The miracle occasioned much arguing among the man's neighbours and acquaintances. But matters really took a turn for the worse when the man was brought to the Pharisees. They went to great lengths to trap him with their clever reasoning, and to convict the Lord Jesus. They fasten on to the fact that the miracle was performed on a Sabbath, and show that they regarded that day as an occasion for doing nothing, rather than doing good.

The man refuses to be frightened by his questioners. His reply under a barrage of questions is classic (verse 25). As Christians there are many questions we cannot answer. Clever people will run rings around us and tie us in all sorts of knots. But one thing only is important—we know what Jesus has done for us.

The aftermath (verses 35-41)

The Pharisees stand condemned. Their pride will not allow them to confess that Christ is the Son of God. On this they prefer to remain blind.

With regard to the man we may notice that his affliction was the means used by God to bring him salvation.

NOTES

The Good Shepherd

THE Gospel according to John contains seven 'I am' sayings. That is, seven utterances of the Lord Jesus are recorded which begin with the words 'I am'. While it would be very wrong for Christians to be emphasizing the importance of their own persons, Jesus Christ never hesitated in directing men's attention to Himself.

The Gate

Although the more familiar figure used in this chapter is that of the Shepherd, we must not forget that Jesus spoke of Himself as the gate or door for the sheep. These words seem to be directed to the Pharisees, who were seeking to gain authority over the Jewish people for themselves. They were really leading people away from God, and therefore Jesus calls them thieves. In order to be true, rather than false teachers of God's people (here called sheep), they needed to submit themselves to Christ, the gate for the sheep. In verse 8 Jesus broadens the scope of His remarks to include everyone. He is the only access men may have to God.

The Shepherd

What makes Jesus not only a Shepherd, but the Good Shepherd? He gives His life for the sheep; it is for the benefit of the sheep that He dies. But how can His death be of benefit to them? Surely only if He dies instead of them. Again, the Good Shepherd never abandons His sheep when danger threatens. The Good Shepherd knows, and is known by, His sheep. The Good Shepherd is determined that others will know of His kindness and He will introduce them into His flock.

What a wonderful Shepherd is the Lord Jesus Christ! He

died on the cross for us. When others who promise to help us and care for us let us down, He never deserts us. His care for us is completely personal. While Paul rejoiced in Christ's death for the world, he also delighted to refer to the Saviour as 'the Son of God, who loved *me*, and gave himself for *me*.' He is still at work saving men and women and bringing them to Himself. What great power He had from His Father, not only to give His life but also to take it again!

Some three months seem to have elapsed between these sayings and those recorded from verse 22 onwards. But the Jews were obviously still smarting as a result of Jesus' words. If they were His sheep they would know many privileges. Probably the greatest of these privileges is that true believers in the Lord Jesus are safe for ever. Sadly, the Jews rejected this privilege.

Let us lean back our souls on these mighty truths, and be thankful. A willing Saviour, a loving Saviour, a Saviour who came specially into the world to bring life to man, is just the Saviour that we need. If we hear His voice, repent and believe, He is our own.   J. C. Ryle

NOTES

16

Jesus Alone with the Twelve

SOME of the Lord Jesus Christ's most remarkable actions and words were reserved for occasions which He shared only with His disciples. This, as we might expect, is especially true of the last meal which He had with the twelve whom He had chosen. Shortly after this He was crucified.

A humble example

Because His love for them meant that He would die for them, Jesus prepared His disciples for life without His bodily presence. He loved them, and love was to govern their conduct. This He demonstrated during their meal, by performing the very menial task of washing the feet of those present, a duty normally assigned to a servant. Pride prevented each of the disciples from doing this. Imagine their astonishment and shame when the Lord Himself moves from one to the other with a towel and basin. Peter's objection is firmly but tenderly answered.

Jesus drives the lesson home. If He whom they call Teacher and Lord is prepared to accept the most humble place, ought not they, His servants, to do likewise? Knowing what they should do is one thing: performing that work is another. There must not be, nor can there be, any place for pride in the Christian's heart.

A surprising revelation

The betrayal of Jesus by Judas takes the disciples by surprise, but not Jesus. He has known all along that one would prove faithless, and has known who that one is. Our Lord prepares the eleven for the act of treachery so that they will not be misled into thinking that He is the helpless victim of Judas' plans, but that they may be certain that God's purpose is being fulfilled.

17

While they wonder who the traitor is, they are taught another very important lesson. It is that they dare not trust themselves. Matthew 26:22 indicates not merely that they suspect one another, but that each one begins to have misgivings about himself. We must never think that we are above, and safe from, committing certain unthinkable sins. Our hearts, says Jeremiah, are deceitful and desperately wicked. We all have a duty at all times to examine ourselves.

A severe warning
After the dismissal of Judas, Jesus speaks of the seriousness of the coming days. The duty to love one another must be uppermost in their thinking, and that love must be similar to the love that the Lord shows to them.

Peter, puzzled and impetuous, declares that he will follow Christ and die for Christ if need be. Seemingly the lessons on pride and self-distrust have swiftly been forgotten. The reply of Jesus made Peter wish he had laid his hand upon his mouth. Fine words are often betrayed by shameful acts. Let Jesus' warning to Peter remind us of our weakness and helplessness.

NOTES

The High-priestly Prayer

THE task of the high priest in the Old Testament was to approach God on behalf of the people. In this chapter we find the Lord Jesus doing just that—representing His people to His Father. We may consider the prayer under three headings.

1. For Himself (verses 1-5)
Although the prayer is chiefly for others, our Lord introduces it by referring to His relationship with His Father. While He was on earth accomplishing salvation for men and women, He surrendered the heavenly enjoyment of unmixed pleasure in His Father's presence. That is now about to be restored to Him. Jesus has magnified His Father on earth by finishing the task He was given. Now let the Father glorify the Son by exalting Him to His rightful place in heaven.

2. For the apostles (verses 6-19)
Jesus' love and concern for His disciples surely come through more clearly here than anywhere. The greatest thing He has done for them is to reveal God to them. He has spoken His Father's words to them, and these they have accepted. He has also protected them and lost none of them. (Although Judas was one of the twelve, he was never really Christ's.)

Jesus stresses that He is praying for His followers, *not* for the world. He prays that the Father should protect them from the devil; that they may know unity amongst themselves; that they may experience the joy of the Lord, and that they may be made holy. In these matters the importance He attaches to God's Word, the Bible, is to be noted (vv.8,14,17).

3. For the church in later days (verses 20-26)
The theme of unity is taken up by the Lord again. It is a unity based upon and similar to the unity that exists between the

Father and the Son. This means that it is not merely an outward display of unity. It is a unity that can exist only among those who are in the Father and the Son, that is, those who have been born from above.

This desired unity has a purpose—a testimony to the unbelieving world. It is through the unity of Christians that men and women are to believe that the Father sent the Son into the world out of love for sinners.

The purpose of this prayer is beautifully stated by the Saviour. It is that those whom the Father has given Him, and for whom He died, may be with Him for ever and may see His glory. To such a prayer, let us say a hearty 'Amen!'

NOTES

The Baptism of Fire

IN Matthew 3:11, John the Baptist said that Jesus would 'baptize you with the Holy Spirit and with fire'. After His resurrection Jesus Himself said virtually the same thing; in Acts 1:5 the phrase 'in a few days' pointed to the fast approaching Day of Pentecost, the facts of which are recorded in Acts 2. On that great day the Christians were baptized with the Holy Spirit and with fire. The purpose of this was that they might have power to witness for Christ in a hostile world.

Very often in Scripture, fire is used as a symbol for the presence of God. This is true over 400 times in the Old Testament and 70 times in the New Testament. (See Isaiah 66:15; 1 Kings 18:24; Hebrews 12:29 and Acts 2:3.)

The need for fire
Seven weeks before Pentecost, the Christians had known the truth of the resurrection. After Christ's ascension they bore the mark of truly regenerate men: 'they worshipped him . . . with great joy' (Luke 24:52). But all this, glorious though it was, was not enough. Jesus said clearly that they still had to receive power. The baptism of fire gave them this power.

If the apostles needed this fire of the Holy Spirit, how much more does the church today! We are saved; we have the truth; we rejoice in the Lord, but is our witness for the Lord powerful and Spirit-led? We need the fire of God.

The supreme need of the church is fire. The baptism of the Spirit is the baptism of fire. Spirit-filled souls are ablaze for God. They love with a love that glows. They believe with a faith that kindles. They serve with a devotion that consumes. They hate sin with a fierceness that burns.

Samuel Chadwick

The result of the fire

For seven weeks the church had the facts of the cross and the resurrection, but they saw no conversions. Facts alone, however glorious and however well-presented, have no converting power. Pentecost set the facts on fire by setting the church on fire. The first result of the fire was that unbelievers heard the wonders of God (v.10); this led to 3,000 being saved (v.41). There is nothing to compare with the power of the Holy Spirit. Peter, who had trembled before the accusation of a serving girl and denied Jesus, now with the fire of God on him preaches fearlessly the glorious gospel.

We mourn over the sin of this nation, but what will change it? Only the gospel preached in the power of the Holy Spirit. That is truth and fire. In 1665 the Great Plague swept through London. Out of the population of 450,000 people, 60,000 died of cholera. Men were powerless to stop this terrible march of death. Then came the Great Fire of London, and the plague fled before the flames. So sin, which seems so permanent and immovable, is banished when the Holy Spirit's fire moves in the human heart.

NOTES

Saul's Conversion

THE apostle Paul was a man who had experienced many remarkable and shattering events in his life. The New Testament tells us of experiences which left an indelible mark upon him: he was shipwrecked (Acts 27); he suffered an earthquake (Acts 16); he was left for dead (Acts 14:19). Events like this are so remarkable that you cannot tell of a man's life and omit them. But there was one outstanding event, of such great importance that the Scripture mentions it not once but three times (in Acts 9, 22 and 26). This was Paul's conversion to Christ on the Damascus road.

What was true of Paul is true of every Christian. Nothing happens to us that can ever approach in importance our conversion. It is the greatest and most significant thing that can ever happen. Why is conversion so important? Because without it no one can know God. Whatever a man may know about God through religion or intellect, he cannot know God as Father and Saviour unless he is converted.

Opposed to Jesus
In Saul of Tarsus we see a man opposed to Jesus. He hated Jesus and all who followed the Saviour (v.1). In his mind and conscience he was not opposed to God, only to Jesus. He actually thought that by persecuting Christians he was pleasing God (Acts 26:9). He was no pagan, no idol-worshipper, no worldly sinner, but rather a devout, God-fearing man who hated Jesus. Whether he knew it or not, opposition to Jesus made him an enemy of God. It is possible to admire Saul's zeal, enthusiasm, sincerity, devout-ness, etc., but they counted for nothing before God. He was opposed to Jesus, and that was the only thing that concerned God. Jesus is the only one who can bring us to God (John

14:6; Acts 4:12; 1 Timothy 2:5). To reject Jesus is to reject God.

Humbled

In Saul's experience on the Damascus road we see three things which are common to all conversions: he was humbled, he was convicted of sin, and he met the living Jesus. Today we are going to consider the first thing. He was humbled.

Saul set out for Damascus full of his own importance, clutching his letters of authority (vv.1,2). Suddenly he is flat on his face (v.4); he has to acknowledge the hated Jesus as Lord (v.5); he is blind and has to be led by the hand (v.8); he desperately needs the help of one of the very Christians he has been persecuting (v.17). It was all most humbling.

The gospel is meant to humble men. Man in sin is always arrogant with regard to God. He thinks he can do without Jesus. Why should he repent? Why does he need the cross and the Saviour's redeeming blood? We think it is all beneath us, and God has to show us how useless and petty we really are. We must be brought to see our great need of Jesus. How hard it was for Saul the Pharisee, the deeply religious man, to have to admit that in reality he was a stranger to God! It is all most humbling, but it is essential to salvation. No one has ever been converted who has not first been humbled.

NOTES

Knowing and Doing

FOR the first time we see the gospel being preached to non-Jews. Jesus had told the disciples (Acts 1:8) to take the message of salvation to the world, but they were very slow to do so. The main reason for this was that the first Christians were Jews, and as Jews they were very prejudiced against Gentiles. This prejudice was so deeply rooted (v.3) that God had to do two remarkable things to remove it.

Peter's vision
The first was Peter's vision and his meeting with Cornelius. The animals Peter saw in the sheet were to the Jews 'unclean' and should not be used for food. His protest (v.8) was in keeping with his Jewish upbringing. God very forcefully rebukes such an attitude (v.9). All this was necessary to prepare Peter to take the gospel to Cornelius, the Roman centurion (Acts 10:22,28), and as a result the nationalistic prejudice of Peter and the other Jewish believers was broken down (v.18). This was a remarkable breakthrough. A new understanding of the breadth of divine love and grace is given to the church.

Persecution
It is one thing to understand something, and another to do it. How does God make sure that they take the gospel to all men? He uses the persecution of their enemies to force them to leave Jerusalem (v.19). But even then we read that they were 'telling the message *only* to Jews' (v.19). In verse 18 they see the truth: in verse 19 they fail to apply it. This is so typical of us today. We can be guilty of such failure in almost every aspect of the Christian life—our money, and the failure to tithe; our time, and the failure to put spiritual things first. We

know what is right, but we do not do it—and what blessing we miss as a consequence!

At last (v.20) some believers preached to non-Jews, and immediately the Lord blessed their ministry with the salvation of a great number of people. These new converts at Antioch were the very first believers to be called CHRISTIANS (v.26). It was a name chosen not by the church but by the pagan society in which they lived.

It has been said that it was a nickname, and that it was given to them as a title of contempt. That may be so . . . I think also, that Antioch named these people by what Antioch saw in them. They were the people of Christ. It was of Christ they spoke, of the Christ they sang, for the Christ they lived. Campbell Morgan

Are you known as a Christian because of your obvious love for the Saviour?

NOTES

A New Continent for Christ

IN this chapter we see the gospel for the first time coming to Europe. Philippi was a city in what we know today as northern Greece. It is clear from verses 6-10 that Paul's visit to this particular city was no accident. God was very much behind it. These are thrilling verses, as we see the Lord opening and closing doors, and slowly but surely pointing His servants in the direction He wants them to go. The Holy Spirit does the same for us today, but we must be sensitive to His leading and anxious to be led.

Different, yet alike
At Philippi we find God bringing the apostle Paul into contact with three souls in need—Lydia, the slave girl and the jailer. Here were three completely different types of people, with nothing in common socially, intellectually or in any other way—except, of course, spiritually, for spiritually they were all sinners and without Christ. Whilst it is true that all are sinners, it is not true that everyone is equally alike in sin. Some sinners are very respectable, some are thieves; some are moral, some immoral. Though the guilt is exactly the same and the condemnation exactly the same, the appearance and experience of sin are different. All are *in sin*, but the *sins* which arise out of the basic sinful nature will vary from one person to another.

This is seen very clearly in the case of Lydia and the jailer. She was a very respectable, religious woman. He was a hard, cruel man of the world. From this chapter we can glean that she had been seeking God for a long time, whilst he had no knowledge of God and no desire for Him. Yet both these people were saved by the grace of God.

What really matters

Salvation is always by grace through faith in Christ, but the means God uses to bring sinners to faith can vary enormously. Lydia was saved very gently as she listened to Paul: 'The Lord opened her heart'. For the jailer it took an earthquake, and a feeling of desperation that made him decide to kill himself. If, years later, these two were asked to give their testimony, one account would be much more dramatic and exciting than the other. Perhaps for that reason the jailer would be asked to give testimony more often than Lydia. But both were saved, and that is all that matters.

Perhaps your conversion was more like Lydia's, and sometimes you are tempted to wish it had been more dramatic. Don't! How you were saved does not matter; how you describe your conversion is unimportant. What really matters above everything else is that you have a conversion to describe.

NOTES

King Agrippa

FOR two years Paul has been kept a prisoner at Caesarea by Governor Felix. Now there is a new governor, Festus, and King Agrippa and his sister, Bernice, come to pay their respects (25:13). Festus discusses Paul with the king, and Agrippa shows great interest and asks to meet the apostle (25:22). The interest is more than casual because the king's full name was Herod Agrippa, and the Herod family had for years behaved violently towards Jesus and His servants. It was Agrippa's great-grandfather who had tried to kill Jesus at His birth (Matthew 2:16); it was his uncle who had murdered John the Baptist (Matthew 14:1-12), and it was his father who had executed James and imprisoned Peter (Acts 12:1-4). Each of these rulers had died suddenly or been disgraced soon after the events mentioned.

A personal challenge
So it was before this man that Paul was brought and given 'permission to speak for yourself' (v.1). But Paul was never interested in speaking merely for himself. He wanted to speak for Christ, and to speak in order to save the soul of Agrippa. Paul acknowledged that the king was 'well acquainted with all the Jewish customs' (v.3) and believed the Scriptures (v.27). Here was a man not ignorant of the basic truths about God, now hearing for the first time the gospel of Jesus Christ. Paul gave his testimony of conversion and proclaimed the need for repentance (v.20). When challenged personally by the apostle (v.27), Agrippa would not give a straight answer (v.28).

A foolish rejection
If you look at various translations, you will see that verse 28 is a difficult one to translate from the original Greek. But

whatever the translation, it is clear that Agrippa rejected the gospel. He came to a correct conclusion about Paul (v.32), but avoided any conclusion about Christ. Why? Because he was more convinced of the fact that the gospel Paul had preached was 'true and reasonable' (v.25) than of the fact that it was biblical (vv.22,23). He could not deny that it was (v.27), but to believe and obey it would involve repentance and he was not prepared for that.

Why would he not repent? Firstly, he held a high position as king and leader of the Jewish community. To become a Christian could mean losing all that. Secondly, there was his sin. With him was Bernice, his sister. Jewish and Roman historians tell us that this brother and sister were living together in vile sin as husband and wife. To become a Christian would certainly mean an end of that relationship. His position and his sin were too important to Agrippa. 'You fool!' says the Bible. 'What good will it be for a man if he gains the whole world, yet forfeits his soul?'

NOTES

The Fall of Man

GOD created Adam and Eve (Genesis 2:7,22) and placed them in the Garden of Eden. In this delightful paradise they had perfect freedom, with only one restriction (2:17). We are immediately reminded of a truth repeated over and over again in Scripture: if man is to live a happy and peaceful life, he must live in harmony with God and in obedience to God's revealed will.

The deception of Satan

There is no greater error than to believe that sin can bring happiness. It is an illusion put into the mind of men by the devil. Satan comes to Eve in the form of a serpent, and his first action is to cast doubt on God's command: 'Did God really say?' (v.1). The emphasis here is on 'really', meaning 'Can it be possible? Are you sure?' In verses 2 and 3 Eve makes it plain that she had correctly understood God's command, and also that she was aware of the consequence of disobedience—'you will die.' Satan flatly contradicts the Word of God—'You will not surely die'—and then goes on to attack the character of God (v.5), implying that He was being selfish in giving such a command.

Satan's lies were believed, and what the Lord had forbidden, Eve now saw as 'good', 'pleasing' and 'desirable' (v.6). She sinned and then involved Adam in her sin.

The reality of sin

It was not long before the so-called pleasures of sin turned sour on them. Firstly, their nakedness bothered them because now their hearts were corrupt (v.7). Secondly, in their guilt they had to hide from God (v.8).

From God they would hide themselves and also from one another. Nor is it merely their nakedness that they would hide. Actually in every aspect of life they must hide something from each other. Sin is secretive and breaks a pure and open fellowship. The blessed communion and companionship of Paradise is shattered, for sin is essentially divisive.   E. J. Young

The consequence of their sin was immediately evident. They were spiritually dead, and this terrible fact is emphasized when they are banished from the presence of God (v.23). Physical death would follow in due course, but spiritual death was immediate.

To see how this affects you, read Romans 5:12. What Adam did has more influence on your life today than anything that is happening now. Your sinful nature is to be traced back to Genesis 3. There is only One who can change your sinful nature and regain for you access to God and peace with God. Read Romans 5:1, 17-19.

NOTES

The Flood

SIN is a very treacherous thing. In Genesis 3 the action of
Adam and Eve does not seem very serious; they merely eat a
fruit. But this was direct rebellion against God, and the seed
sown in Genesis 3 comes to full flower in the terrible
condition described in verse 5 of this chapter. The holy God
of heaven looks down on the world He has created and sees
'evil all the time'. His reaction is inevitable (vv.6,7). This is
the way that the holy God always reacts to sin. It grieves Him
deeply and the terrible judgment of verse 7 is entirely just.
The instrument of divine judgment is the Flood, but the
Flood did not come immediately.

There was one man who found favour with the Lord. Noah
was a righteous man, a godly man, one who loved the Lord
and obeyed Him. The goodness of this man was a further
condemnation on the rest of mankind. It left them without
any excuse. If Noah could love and serve God, so could they.

Grace and mercy

God, in His grace and mercy, provided for Noah and his
family a salvation. Noah is instructed to build an Ark
(vv.14-22). Every detail is given to him, and so this
God-designed refuge is the perfect shape to provide just what
Noah needs. It was very like a modern day barge, built more
to float than to sail. The questions are always asked: Did the
Flood really take place? Was there a Noah's Ark? To the
Bible-believing Christian there is no doubt of the truth of this
story. It is not a myth, but fact. If you wish to study this
more, obtain a book that is fairly easy to read called *Myths
and Miracles* by David C. C. Watson, or else a far more
detailed book, *The Genesis Flood*, by Morris and Whitcomb.

Grace and judgment

When Noah was safely in the Ark, the judgment began. There were forty days and forty nights of rain (7:12) until every sinner was destroyed under the flood waters. Some may say, 'How cruel of God!' If you read the chapter carefully, however, you see that, terrible though the wrath of God is, He is also a God slow to anger and abundant in mercy. There is grace as well as judgment in this story.

When God saw men 'evil all the time', He pronounced judgment on them and said, 'My Spirit will not contend with man for ever' (v.3). But the Holy Spirit did not stop showing man his sin and guilt immediately, for God in His great mercy gave the world another 120 years to repent (v.3). During this time Noah preached to people; the apostle Peter calls him 'a preacher of righteousness' (2 Peter 2:5). For 120 years men refused the grace of God and took lightly the warning of coming judgment. A suspended sentence is not a pardon; judgment delayed is not judgment escaped. The terrible thing is that man has still not learned the lesson of the Flood. Read Matthew 24:36-41.

NOTES

The Happy Man

THE first psalm shows us very clearly the difference between the Christian and everyone else. The Christian is the 'blessed man'—the truly happy man. This happy state is not the result of temperament or circumstances, but a direct consequence of his relationship to the Lord.

What he does not do (v.1)
He does not trifle with sin: he does not take his 'counsel'—his advice, ambition, direction—from the wicked. Neither does he 'stand in the way of sinners'—that is, he refuses to identify himself with them. Further, he has no sympathy with those who mock or scorn the things of God—he does not 'sit in the seat of mockers'.

Here we have a man who is opposed to sin in its every shape and form. Some would say that to be like this will make you a miserable, stiff character. Not at all. The pleasures of sin are deceptive, and do not bring lasting happiness. True happiness is only to be found in communion with God.

What he does (v.2)
Note the word 'delight': it speaks of something more than duty or habit. This certainly does not come naturally, but as a result of being given a new heart. The Christian takes no pleasure in sin, but finds great delight in the law of God. For the Psalmist, the law of God meant little more than the first five books of the Bible. How much more do we have cause to rejoice in the whole of revealed Scripture!

Such delight causes the Christian not merely to read the Bible occasionally, but to meditate upon it day and night. To meditate means to 'ponder, consider, give time to think upon'. How much time do *you* give to the study of the Word of God?

Meditation is a spiritual index. The index shows what is in a book, so meditation shows what is in the heart.

Thomas Watson

The result

The result of such a life is spiritual stability and fruitfulness (v.3). More than that, it is a life that pleases God, so that He watches over it (v.6). The Lord is constantly protecting and guiding such a person, so that 'whatever he does prospers' (v.3). That does not mean, however, that he is without troubles and problems, for it is *spiritual* and not material prosperity that is ours in Christ.

Compare with this the description of ungodly men (vv.4-6). They are 'like chaff'—worthless; they are 'blown away'—they have no stability; they will 'perish'—there is no salvation.

NOTES

Forsaken

THIS is a Messianic psalm: that is, it is a psalm which speaks of the coming Messiah or Christ. David wrote the words, and they recount his own experiences; but at the same time, and more importantly, under the inspiration of the Holy Spirit the Psalmist speaks clearly of Jesus Christ on the cross.

Before us we have a description both of the darkness and of the glory of the cross, the suffering of Christ and the glory which shall follow. O for grace to draw near and see this great sight!   C. H. Spurgeon

Forsaken by God (vv.1-5)

The opening words of the psalm were uttered by our Saviour on the cross (Matthew 27:46). He was not merely quoting Scripture, but was actually experiencing what that verse spoke of: His heavenly Father was turning His back on Him. The Holy One (v.3), who had helped and delivered His people on many occasions (vv.4,5), now forsakes His only begotten Son. Why? Because Jesus was on the cross as our sin-bearer, facing the wrath of God. He was there as 'a sacrifice of atonement' or 'a propitiation' (Romans 3:25), to turn away divine wrath from the guilty sinner He represented.

The death that Jesus died was full of horror, and no understanding of the atonement can be satisfactory which does not reckon with that. It is the terrible nature of the death that He died that is significant, and not merely the fact that He died.   Leon Morris

The loneliness and agony of the cross (vv.6-21)

Remember that Jesus is the Lord of glory, 'the exact representation' of God's glory (Hebrews 1:3); yet see the description of Him now in verse 6. It was human sin that caused this. Read Matthew 27:41-44, and marvel at how accurate a description this psalm presents to us (vv.7,8). Now read very slowly and thoughtfully verses 12-21 in the psalm, and ponder on the sufferings of Jesus that purchased your salvation. We see men's hatred of Christ; but more than that, we see God's hatred of sin. Sin is an insult to the holiness of God; it separates man from God and leaves him without hope and without comfort in a world which is hostile to God. All this we see Jesus enduring on the cross as the sinner's representative.

Deliverance (vv.22-31)

The transition is very marked: from a horrible tempest all is changed into calm.   C. H. Spurgeon

Calvary is passed, and something of Christ's triumph is now revealed. The lament of verse 1 turns into the joyful assurance of verse 24. The forsaking was only temporary, and now sweet communion is once again being enjoyed with the heavenly Father. The result is praise (v.22), reverence (v.23), satisfaction (v.26), worship (v.29).

NOTES

The Shepherd

THIS psalm of David, the shepherd boy of Bethlehem, holds a place in the heart of Christians unrivalled by almost any other portion of Scripture. There is a depth of meaning in every sentence, and a rich variety of experience in every verse. David's experience in this psalm is one that every true Christian longs for, and so, almost instinctively, we make Psalm 23 a prayer. To David, however, it is not a prayer for what he wants, but a song of thanksgiving for what he already has.

David's experience

A psalm like this makes us realize how little we really know of God. We can rejoice in our salvation, but how much do we know of the close walk with God that David obviously rejoices in? Psalm 23 is the prayer of many Christians, but the *experience* of very few. How do we make it our experience?

We have to realize that this close fellowship with God *is* possible for us. There are Christians who are so conscious of their sin and so depressed by a sense of their unworthiness that they feel they will never know the joyful assurance David shows. They know the truth of the first statement, 'The Lord is my shepherd'—they know they are saved. They know the truth of the last statement, 'I will dwell in the house of the Lord for ever'—they know they can never lose their salvation. Somehow, however, they have little or no experience of what lies between these two great statements. Unlike the Psalmist, they seem to lack so many things (v.1); they are very unsure about God guiding them (vv.2,3); death terrifies them (v.4)—and so on.

Our problem

The problem is that the despondent Christian allows his sense of unworthiness, which rightly hinders him from trusting himself, to prevent him from trusting God. If we can truly say, 'The Lord is my shepherd', then we ought to be able to say everything else in the psalm. The entire psalm simply spells out in detail the meaning of that first statement. If we are saved, in a right relationship to Almighty God, then He will be with us in all situations.

Its cure

We live far too much upon our spiritual feelings. We get greatly elated when we see signs of spiritual growth in our lives, and greatly depressed when we see sin triumphing in us. To all such Christians, Psalm 23 says, 'Fix your faith not so much on what *you* do for God, but on what *God* is doing for you.' Notice that throughout the psalm David is taking delight in what the Lord is doing for him. It is true that the Bible teaches us to examine ourselves, but we are never meant to stop at that. We are to rejoice in the goodness and mercy of God, which follow us every day not because of what we do, but because the Lord is our Shepherd.

NOTES

God's Way

THIS chapter presents to us in very clear terms God's way of salvation.

I know of no chapter in the Bible which states so clearly and so perfectly at one and the same time the essential evangelistic message for the unbeliever and the status and privileges of the believer.   D. M. Lloyd-Jones

What we were (vv. 1-3)
Here is God's view of man. It is not a pretty picture, but it is an accurate description of all men outside of Christ: they are dead in sin; disobedient; in bondage to the ruler of the kingdom of the air (the devil). Notice that in verse 3 Paul says this is true of all of us. There is no exception, and this state of sin brings everyone under the wrath of God.

Man is like this not by accident, not by circumstance, not by upbringing or environment, but by nature. Man's nature is corrupt and hostile to God. The permissive society is only human nature doing what it enjoys doing—living with a disregard for God and bowing to Satan's influence.

What God did for us (vv. 4-18)
Sin makes man's position hopeless (v. 12). The gospel is the good news of what God has done to break the power of sin in man's life and bring the sinner to eternal salvation. There are many great words in this passage: mercy, grace, faith, blood, reconcile, peace, access. Each of these words in a special way spells out to us the wonder of God's great love. Here is a God great in love, rich in mercy, who saves hopeless, helpless, undeserving sinners. How does God save us? Count the

number of times CHRIST is mentioned in these verses. It is through Christ that this great love and rich mercy come to us. Salvation is by grace (undeserved favour) through faith in what Christ Jesus did for us on the cross.

What we are in Christ (vv.19-22)
Contrast these amazing four verses with the opening three verses. It is the same people Paul is describing, but now they are Christians. What a difference! They are God's now, not Satan's; they are saved from the power and guilt of sin. The bridge between these two extreme positions is the grace of God, and it is the *only* bridge.

NOTES

Light and Darkness

THE great difference we saw in Ephesians 2, which is the result of God's grace, has now got to be seen in the ordinary day-to-day life of the Christian. We are living in a world of darkness, but we are to live as children of light (v.8). This is not easy. Read verses 3 and 4. It does not matter whether you are at school or at work, you are daily confronted with sexual immorality, impurity, greed, obscenity and coarse joking. It is very easy to be drawn into this; after all, not very long ago it was natural to you. But now you are a Christian and there must 'not be even a hint' of these things about you. Light and darkness are incompatible; they cannot live together. The Christian is to 'have nothing to do with the fruitless deeds of darkness' (v.11).

All this may seem an impossible task to a new Christian, but we are given help and encouragement.

The Lord's will (v.17)
In order to avoid sin we must 'understand what the Lord's will is' (v.17), and we must set ourselves to 'find out what pleases the Lord' (v.10). This inevitably takes us to the Scriptures. 'How can a young man keep his way pure? By living according to your word' (Psalm 119:9). Make the Bible your daily delight. Read it and meditate on its message. Get to know the mind of God through the inspired writings.

The Spirit's filling (v.18)
The Holy Spirit

really does stimulate. He does not merely appear to do so, as alcohol does, and thereby fools and deludes us. The Holy Spirit is an active, positive, real stimulus.

D. M. Lloyd-Jones

We all need to be filled with the Holy Spirit, not just in order to live a supercharged spiritual life, but for the everyday encounters. Notice how Paul goes on immediately in 5:22-6:9 to deal with how the Christian should behave as wife, husband, child, parent, employee and employer. Read these verses slowly and thoughtfully. Is this how you are living? You need the power of the Holy Spirit to do so. Then, having got to know God's will, seek the enabling of the Holy Spirit to live to God's glory. How can we be filled with the Spirit?

I believe the answer to the question 'How can I be filled?' may be answered in four words, all of them active verbs. They are these: (1) surrender (2) ask (3) obey (4) believe.

A. W. Tozer

NOTES

The Armour of God

THE Christian life is a battle—make no mistake about that. The moment you became a Christian you made a deadly enemy, who never stops trying to ruin your relationship with Christ.

Your enemy
Your enemy is the devil (vv.11,12). He is no ordinary enemy: his power and influence are enormous, and his agents span the whole world. Even Jesus calls him the prince of this world (John 14:30). To know that the devil is against you can be a frightening prospect. What are you to do? Surrender or fight? Read 1 John 5:18 and James 4:7. Here is encouragement: you can know victory over this terrible foe. How?

Your strength
'Be strong in the Lord' (v.10). Quite rightly, you feel that of yourself you have no strength for the battle. God knows this, and therefore He supplies all the strength and power you need. The strength of the Lord has already defeated Satan. It is a proved power, and it is yours in Christ.

God's armour
God supplies a wonderful armour for the battle:

The belt of truth—a knowledge of and belief in the truth of Scripture. This protects the mind.

The breastplate of righteousness—the righteousness we have in Christ (read Philippians 3:9). This protects the heart.

Your feet fitted with . . . the gospel of peace—peace with God. This gives us stability.

The shield of faith—faith that rests in the promises of God. This extinguishes the arrows of doubt Satan hurls at you.

The helmet of salvation—an awareness of your salvation. This keeps you going when the battle gets hot.

The sword of the Spirit—the Word of God, the Bible (read Psalm 119:15,16,105).

It is God who supplies the armour, but *you* must put it on (v.13). If you are knowing constant defeat in your Christian life, it is because you are not daily putting on the armour of God. 'Putting on' involves discipline and obedience. Daily Bible study and prayer (vv.18-20), regular fellowship with other Christians, attendance at Sunday worship and mid-week prayer meetings—these are all part of putting on the armour, so that you can fight and defeat Satan. Particular emphasis is laid here on prayer. Prayer is essential for spiritual growth and strength. There is no substitute for it.

Prayer must buckle on all the other parts of our Christian armour. We must join prayer with all these graces, for our defence against these spiritual enemies, imploring help and assistance of God, as the case requires: we must pray always.   Matthew Henry

NOTES

Pressures

NEBUCHADNEZZAR and his army had invaded Israel and completely defeated the people of God. The majority of the nation were taken from their homeland into captivity in Babylon. King Nebuchadnezzar ordered that the best young men among the captives be brought to the palace so that they may be trained to serve him (vv.3-6). Among them were four boys, possibly in their late teens, Daniel, Hananiah, Mishael and Azariah.

Brainwashing (vv.3-7)
This order of the king's was a very clever move to control the minds of the future leaders of Israel.

> *This, then, is none other than a grim plan of in-doctrination—or if you like the modern term, brain-washing. They were told not only what they must eat and drink, they were going to be told also what they must think. They were going to be taught the learning of the Chaldeans. It is a complete take-over bid of re-education, by which they are to be utterly and permanently changed.*
>
> James Philip

Even their names (v.7) were changed from God-honouring ones to names which honoured idols. See what their names meant:

Daniel ('God is my judge') is changed to Belteshazzar ('Bel protect his life')

Hananiah ('God has been gracious') becomes Shadrach ('inspiration of Rach')

Mishael ('who is of God') is called Meshach ('who is this?')

Azariah ('God has helped') becomes Abednego ('servant of the god Nabu')

The pressures were certainly on these boys to forget God and conform to the pagan ways of Babylon. And it was all done so subtly. It is still the same today. The world never ceases to attempt to turn people away from God. Young Christians in particular face tremendous pressures to conform to the ways of the world. Never minimize, or discount as unimportant, anything that happens in your life that can in any way affect your relationship with God. The wiles of Satan are often more dangerous than his thunderbolts.

Faithful (vv.8-21)
How do you cope with these pressures? Do what Daniel did (v.8). He resolved, he was determined, not to give in, and he and his three friends remained faithful while many other young Israelites conformed. You do not remain faithful by being indifferent, undisciplined or casual: you must resolve, you must determine to be so. Such faithfulness is a costly business. It cost these four the luxury of living like kings (v.5), and meant that, instead, they lived for three years on vegetables and water (v.16).

It is costly being a Christian in an alien world, but our God is no man's debtor. He blesses and rewards such faithfulness. See in this chapter God's mercies to Daniel, Hananiah, Mishael and Azariah (vv.19,20). Read also Mark 10:28-30.

NOTES

Faithfulness

YESTERDAY we saw Daniel as a teenager, but in today's reading he is a very old man. Whether young or old, however, the outstanding virtue of faithfulness marks the life of this man of God. What exactly does it mean to be faithful?

Faithful before God
First of all—and this must always be first—he was faithful in his dealings with God. Three times every day he prayed and gave thanks to God (v.10). No Christian can be faithful who does not know regular daily communion with God in prayer. It does not matter if it is once or twice or three times, but there must be daily prayer. If you are too busy to pray, then you are *too* busy. This must be the top priority in the Christian's life. Faithfulness starts with our own personal communion with God, but it does not end there.

Faithful before men
Verses 3 and 4 describe Daniel at his daily work. He had a good job and was in line for promotion (v.3), for he was a man of exceptional ability. Perhaps you are not like that, but as a Christian it should be said of you that 'he was trustworthy and neither corrupt nor negligent' (v.4). This has nothing to do with ability, but it has all to do with character. It means that as a Christian you may not be the brightest pupil in the class, but you ought to be the hardest worker; you may not be the most skilful person in the factory, but you ought to be the most trustworthy and reliable. Your Christian character must show in everyday life. In today's society, where corruption and idleness dominate life, the Christian should stand out, as did Daniel, as a model of integrity and faithfulness.

Such a quality of life makes an inevitable impact on those around. Read Matthew 5:13-16.

God's faithfulness
The devil hates to see a life that brings praise to God, and does all he can to oppose it. Daniel's life aroused the intense jealousy of his enemies, and they plotted his downfall (vv.4-9). It looked as if they were going to succeed, until God intervened (v.21).

Here is the extraordinary thing: by remaining faithful and because of this, by being cast into the lions' den . . . Daniel effectively escaped from the greater lion he was facing. By facing him (that is, the devil), he escaped him. This is the glorious paradox . . . Listen to Peter, 'Be sober, be vigilant; because . . . the devil, as a roaring lion, walketh about, seeking whom he may devour; whom resist stedfast in the faith' (1 Peter 5:8,9). James Philip

Now read James 4:7.

NOTES

The Excellent Way

IN chapter twelve Paul has been considering the nature of spiritual gifts. At the end of the chapter he urges Christians to seek the better gifts. The way to do this is the way of love. Paul's understanding of love goes far beyond the best meaning that we normally give to love. Christian love is of a different order from the highest ideal of human love. This chapter sets out perfectly what the Christian understands by love.

The necessity of love (vv.1-3)
The most striking and remarkable claims a man can make are empty claims if the man has no love. He may create a great impression by displays of speaking in other languages, of prophesying, of generosity, and even of sacrifice, but unless his conduct is inspired by love, it brings him no profit. His words and claims will not ring true, and his actions will be worthless. Love is the essential ingredient in any Christian experience.

The expression of love (vv.4-7)
Love shows itself in a number of ways. Notice that none of these is eye-catching or spectacular. Love never shouts out 'Here I am! Look at me!' Patience, kindness, love of the truth are the virtues by which love is recognized. But it is also known by the fact that vices such as arrogance and selfishness are absent. Perhaps above all, we may draw attention to the constancy we find in love—it 'always' behaves in the same manner.

Think of what that person must be like who fits the description in verses 4-7. Is there such a person? Has there ever been one? Yes—but only one. Are not these qualities a beautiful outline of the Person and life of our Lord Jesus Christ? Let us strive to be like our Saviour.

The permanence of love (vv.8-13)

Love lasts for ever. The gifts the Corinthians boasted of—speaking in other languages, prophesying—would all one day come to an end. In heaven there will be no need of these. They belong to the present, not to the future. Now we are compared to children growing to manhood. When we arrive at manhood, childlike features and behaviour are out of place. So, in heaven, the imperfect features of our life on earth are left behind. Again, now we are compared to those who see a likeness, a reflection; in heaven we shall be like those who see plainly, and the need for the mirror will be gone. Even these gifts, which are useful on earth, will vanish away.

Faith, hope, love go on when all the others fail. And amongst these three, the chief is love.

Whereas the best concept of love before the New Testament was that of a love for the best one knows, the Christians thought of love as that quality we see displayed in the cross. It is a love for the utterly unworthy, a love which proceeds from a God who is love. It is a love lavished upon others without a thought of whether they are worthy to receive it or not. It proceeds rather from the nature of the lover, than from any merit in the beloved. Leon Morris

NOTES

The Resurrection of the Dead

THERE are certain chapters of the Bible that are immediately identified with particular subjects. This chapter is one to which Christians invariably turn when thinking of the question of the resurrection. It does not say all that there is to say on this important matter, but it does develop and state the doctrine of the resurrection more fully than any other portion of the Word of God. Paul deals with the subject here because there were some in Corinth who, alarmingly, were denying that the dead would rise.

The resurrection of Christ (vv.1-19)
This is absolutely basic. That Christ arose from the dead is an essential part of the gospel Paul preached. Notice Paul's appeal to the authority of the Scriptures (vv.3,4). That the Lord did rise is established by witness that Paul considers undeniable (vv.5-8).

If Christ did not rise from the dead, certain dreadful consequences follow: the preaching of the apostles is worthless, the apostles themselves are liars, Christian faith is in vain, and those who claim to possess such faith remain with their sins unforgiven. Worst of all, those Christians who have already died are lost. Our hopes all end with death.

The resurrection of believers (vv.20-34)
The resurrection of Christ is in fact the guarantee of the resurrection of all Christians. Every human being is a descendant of Adam, is 'in Adam', and therefore dies. Every Christian is 'in Christ', and therefore will be made alive. Just as death comes through Adam, the resurrection comes through Christ. The resurrection will signal the end, when

Christ's victory over all His enemies will be complete and apparent to everyone.

Some people in Corinth were being baptized for the dead. Mormons still practise this. Paul uses this misguided practice to indicate the uselessness of being baptized for the dead, if the dead perish. Similarly, why do the apostles court danger, if there is no resurrection?

The resurrection body (vv.35-58)
What sort of bodies will we have? Just as a seed, when it is sown, gives rise to a plant, so the body that dies and is buried is raised in another form. Although the one comes from the other, there are certain contrasts between the two bodies. These Paul points out.

The bodies we now have cannot enter heaven. They must be changed—and they will be! The glorious transformation will take place at the sound of the last trumpet. In the light of the assurance given them of their future, Paul exhorts the Christians to faithfulness in Christ's service.

Paul argues that those who deny the bodily resurrection of believers virtually deny Christ's resurrection and empty the faith of its saving content.   Geoffrey B. Wilson

NOTES

Mind How You Speak

SOME of the people to whom James wrote his letter wanted to be teachers and public speakers in the matters of God's Word. The *New Bible Commentary* says that they failed to recognize that 'the fundamental qualification for teaching is learning.' All who speak publicly carry great responsibility, because of the effect produced by their words. Although what James has to say is directed mainly at such people, it is easy to see that what he writes can be and must be applied to us all. Indeed the warning of this chapter is one of the most serious in the whole Bible.

Beware!
So anxious is James to direct attention to the harmful use of the tongue that he uses no less than six illustrations:
1. *Bits and horses.* All that is needed to turn the horse in any direction is to use the bit.
2. *Rudders and ships.* Great vessels, driven by the force of the winds, can yet be controlled by a small rudder.
3. *Sparks and forests.* Huge forest fires are kindled by little sparks.

The bit, the rudder and the spark, have an effect out of proportion to their size. What good or harm can result from skilful or careless application of them! Your tongue is small, but consider the immense influence it has!
4. *Men and creatures.* Man's power can be seen in the dominion he has over animals. Man has tamed and can tame the most unruly creatures. But he cannot control his own tongue!
5. *Springs and water.* No fountain sends out both fresh and salt water.

6. *Trees and fruit.* No tree can produce more than one kind of fruit.

How absurd then for the same tongue now to praise God, then to curse God's image in man!

True wisdom
Toward the end of the chapter, James deals with the subject of wisdom. Would-be teachers must possess this. But there are two kinds of wisdom, each having its own origin, character and effect:

One is from heaven, the other from the devil.

One shows purity, humility, understanding, meekness, mercy: the other shows envy, selfishness, falsehood.

One produces righteousness, the other chaos and wickedness.

Finally, may we not say that true wisdom consists in large measure in control of the tongue? Are you wise?

On the one hand, to control the tongue is to control the whole person [v.2], and on the other hand, what happens in our tongue is an index of what the heart is like [v.12]. The bitter fruit of words proceeds from the corrupt root of the heart.   J.A. Motyer

NOTES

Life and Light

IN the first epistle of John, three matters constantly recur:
1. *What do Christians believe?* 2. *Do they love one another?*
3. *What kind of lives do they lead?* These questions are asked
as tests of whether we are truly born again. If we are, we will
believe what the Bible says and what the apostles teach
(especially concerning the Lord Jesus), we will love one
another, and we will live a life above criticism. In this opening
chapter, two of these three subjects are introduced.

Who is Jesus?
One of the reasons why John wrote was to deal with certain
people who were heretics. They were teaching untruths
concerning the Saviour. They denied that He, the eternal Son
of God, had actually become man. John's emphasis is that
Christ has actually revealed Himself to him and the other
disciples through their three principal senses—they saw Him,
heard Him and touched Him. There could be no possible
doubt that He was a man. But more than this, Jesus is the
eternal Son of God (v.3). He is the Word of life (v.1). This
cannot be perceived by our senses; it must be perceived by
faith and is essential to our having a living relationship with
God and enjoying fellowship with other believers.

Walking in the light
There are two great statements made by John in his writings.
The first and most familiar is that God is love. Here we have
the second, not so well-known, but equally important: God is
light. Now if we claim to belong to Him, we must reflect His
character. Sin must never be the chief and directing factor in
our lives. We will live lives pleasing to God. This John calls
walking in the light.

John does not teach, nor does the New Testament anywhere teach, that we shall be without sin, or perfect in this life, before we arrive in heaven. Fellowship does not mean sinlessness, since it is while we enjoy fellowship that the blood of Jesus Christ goes on cleansing us. If we were without sin, there would be no need for this continual purifying. Moreover, if we claim to be without sin, we deceive ourselves, we lie, and, worst of all, we make God a liar. Although we are aware of the presence of sin, we must never be under its power and control.

Verse 9 sets before us the path of forgiveness, and is one of the most glorious promises in the Bible. See that you rest upon it.

The purpose of the proclamation of the gospel is, therefore, not salvation but fellowship. Yet, properly understood, this is the meaning of salvation in its widest embrace, including reconciliation to God in Christ . . . holiness of life (see verse 6), and incorporation in the Church ('ye . . . with us'). This fellowship is the meaning of eternal life. John R. W. Stott

NOTES

Spiritual Conflict

Although David is not mentioned as the author, this psalm must be the offspring of his pen: it is so Davidic, it smells of the son of Jesse, it bears the marks of his style and experience in every letter . . . it is the voice of a spiritual believer under depressions, longing for the renewal of the divine presence, struggling with doubts and fears, but yet holding his ground by faith in the living God.
C. H. Spurgeon

The sorrow of a godly soul (vv.3,4)
David has been driven from his home and from the house of God. He is in the wilderness, under severe spiritual affliction and conflict. Tears flow easily and continually as his enemies mock him with the taunt 'Where is your God?' and claim that God has forsaken him. Read 2 Samuel 16:7,8. There is no sympathy from the world when the Lord's people feel low and distressed.

The pain is increased as David remembers more blessed times. Remembering can be harmful or good, depending upon our spiritual state and why we look back. If we wallow in what used to be, then we will finish up like David in verse 4, depressed and dejected.

The desire of a godly soul (vv.1,2)
David's desire is not for restoration to the palace or to power, nor even for revenge: it is an overwhelming desire for God. He is like a deer being chased by hunters, whose mouth is dry, and who pants for water to give him renewed strength to escape. The deer's need is not casual but desperate in the extreme. So is David's thirst for God. He wants to know

again the refreshing presence of God, the living God. It is
only the living God who can satisfy the thirst of a godly soul.

The hope of a godly soul (vv.5,6)
David's faith reasons with his fear; his hope argues with his
sorrows. He is in trouble physically and spiritually, but that is
not new. He has known similar situations before and the Lord
has always delivered him, so he has great grounds for hope.
What God has done, He can do again. He is unchangeable,
therefore His grace and mercy are the strongest grounds for
hope. As this is realized, assurance returns—'for I will yet
praise him'.

When you feel downcast and the spiritual conflict almost
overwhelms you, do what David did: 'Put your hope in God.'

NOTES

Penitence

TO understand this psalm you must first read 2 Samuel, chapters 11 and 12. There we read of David's terrible sin, and of Nathan the prophet confronting him with his guilt. Psalm 51 is David's prayer of repentance to God.

Confession of sin (vv.3-6)

He makes no excuses: it is *my* transgression, *my* sin. We can never blame anyone else for our sin, though we often try to do so. Sin is our personal responsibility, and even though (as verse 5 correctly teaches us) we are sinners by nature, each separate act of sin is our own deliberate rebellion against the law of God. David had very clearly sinned against Uriah, but here he acknowledges that all sin is against God (v.4). This is a very solemn thought. The poison of sin lies in its opposition to Almighty God, and when we sin against each other, we are sinning against God.

So David confesses his personal guilt (v.3), his corrupt nature (v.5) and his rebellion against God (v.4).

Prayer for pardon (vv.1,2,7-12)

Confession is an indispensable condition of pardon (1 John 1:9), but God forgives not merely because we confess. David knew this and so he does not pray, 'Pardon me because I confess my guilt.' Neither does he say to God, 'You ought to pardon me because previously I have not sinned very much' (1 Kings 15:5). His hope for pardon rests in the mercy, unfailing love and great compassion of the Lord (vv.1,2).

Sin pollutes and leaves an ugly stain, and so the sinner must be washed and cleansed, and the sin blotted out. Hyssop (v.7) was a little shrub with which the blood and water of purification were applied under the Law of God (Numbers 19:2-6, Hebrews 9:19). So David is asking God to cleanse him by the means He has provided. God's appointed means to deal with our sin is the precious blood of the Lord Jesus Christ (Hebrews 9:14).

> *O that some reader may take heart, even now while smarting under sin, to do the Lord the honour to rely thus confidently on the finished sacrifice of Calvary and the infinite mercy there revealed.*　　　　C. H. Spurgeon

Remember that Psalm 51 is the prayer of a child of God. In other words, here is the repentance of a converted man. Repentance is not merely an experience necessary to salvation; it is the Christian's experience throughout life when he is aware of sin. 'The thing David had done displeased the Lord' (2 Samuel 11:27). Have you displeased the Lord? If so, confess it and pray for pardon.

NOTES

Faith on Trial

The 73rd Psalm deals with a problem that has often perplexed and discouraged God's people. It is a double problem—why should the godly frequently have to suffer, especially in view of the fact that the ungodly frequently appear to be most prosperous?   D. M. Lloyd-Jones

Here we have the experience of a man of God. It is not a very pleasant experience, but one that is all too common. The man has a problem, and as a result his faith is beginning to waver (v.2).

He looks at ungodly men (vv.3-12)
These people have no time for God; they even mock the Almighty (v.11). Yet they prosper in life and seem to be free from the many problems and trials which trouble God's people. This man of God begins to envy them, and to hanker after the prosperity and peace that they enjoy. He is beginning to slide.

He looks at himself (vv.13,14)
He begins to feel sorry for himself, and concludes that it is a waste of time trying to live a godly and righteous life. Self-pity is one of the most destructive forces in a Christian's life. The moment you begin to indulge it, the downward slide is accelerated.

He looks again at the ungodly (vv.16-20)
For the first time he is considering *all* the facts. He goes to the sanctuary of God and is reminded that life is more than mere temporary pleasure and success. Man is an eternal being, answerable to Almighty God. These ungodly men, whose

lives seem so solid and strong, are really on very slippery ground (v.18). They appear to have much, but in reality they have nothing because they do not have God. Read Matthew 16:26 and Luke 12:13-21.

He looks again at himself (vv.21-28)

His slide into despair has been arrested. How? Because he is held by the hand of a loving and gracious God (v.23). He realizes how sinful his envy was, and now he begins to evaluate his true riches as a child of God (vv.23-28). The supreme blessing is to be near God (v.28).

> *I'd rather have Jesus than silver or gold,*
> *I'd rather be His than have riches untold,*
> *I'd rather have Jesus than houses or land,*
> *I'd rather be led by His nail-pierced hand:*
> > *Than to be the king of a vast domain,*
> > *And be held in sin's dread sway,*
> > *I'd rather have Jesus than anything*
> > *This world affords today.*

NOTES

Praise the Lord

THE book of Psalms is like a range of mountains with 150 peaks reaching up from earth and pointing to God. Each psalm makes its own contribution to our knowledge of God, but inevitably here and there along this divine range there are peaks which stand out in grandeur. Psalm 103 is one of these. It has been called 'the Everest of the Psalms'. It does not contain a single prayer or a single petition, but it is simply filled with praise for the character of God. Here we are told that our God is:

A forgiving God (vv.3,4)
Notice that He forgives *all* sins. What a comfort this is to depraved sinners, bound by the chains of a sinful nature!

A gracious God (v.8)
He forgives because He is compassionate and gracious. Our sins deserve judgment and hell, but in grace He does not treat us as we deserve.

A loving God (v.11)
Who can describe the love of God? Even the description in this verse is inadequate to describe a love that is as great and immense as God Himself. Yet it is a love especially demonstrated to those who fear Him (vv.11,13,17). This is not the fear of terror, but refers rather to a sense of awe and wonder and reverence for an amazing God.

A sovereign God (v.19)
Our God reigns. He is the almighty, omnipotent, sovereign God. His throne is established; it can never be moved, not by all the evil and sin in the world.

This matchless sovereignty is the pledge of our security, the pillar on which our confidence may safely lean.

C. H. Spurgeon

Go on through the psalm and see the greatness and glory of your God. The only proper reaction to this in a Christian is to praise the Lord. If the angels and heavenly hosts have cause to praise God, how much more do we! As those who have been 'Ransomed, healed, restored, forgiven', we do not need to look for reasons to praise God, though there are plenty of them. The very *character* of God is reason for praise, and the blessings of salvation should merely serve to amplify the praise that is continually in our hearts.

'Praise the Lord, O my soul; all my inmost being, praise his holy name.'

NOTES

The Passover

THE historic event of the Passover was one of the most momentous in Jewish history. It was never to be forgotten (vv.14,24). For 430 years they had been in Egypt, and for much of that time they had been slaves. Pharaoh, the ruler of Egypt, was loath to lose all these slaves, and despite the plagues the Lord brought upon the land (Exodus 7-10) he refused to release them. But no man can resist the almighty God, and the Lord brings to Egypt the most terrible plague of all, the death of the firstborn (Exodus 11:4,5). Divine judgment was to visit the land.

The blood of the lamb

Every household would feel its effects, but the Lord makes a distinction between His people and the Egyptians (11:7). That distinction was the blood of the lamb (vv.12,13). There were many details the Israelites had to obey (vv.3-11), but by far the most important was with reference to the blood. The Lord said, 'when I see the blood, I will pass over you' (v.13).

The institution and ritual of the Passover supply us with one of the most striking and blessed foreshadowments of the cross-work of Christ to be found anywhere in the Old Testament. Its importance may be gathered from the frequency with which the title 'Lamb' is afterwards applied to the Saviour, a title which looks back to what is before us in Exodus 12.   A. W. Pink

Our Passover Lamb

Christ, says Paul in 1 Corinthians 5:7, is 'our Passover Lamb'. Peter says the same thing when he teaches that our redemption comes only through 'the precious blood of

Christ, a lamb without blemish or defect' (1 Peter 1:19). Compare that with verse 5 in Exodus 12. What both apostles are saying is that Jesus does for us what the Passover lamb did for the Jews. Just as the blood of the lamb on the doorpost delivered them from the judgment which the angel of death was bringing, so the blood of Christ delivers sinners from the power of divine justice. Christ died for us, and God's judgment passes over us. This is the reason why the New Testament writers speak of salvation through Christ's blood, and not simply of His death:

> *The term **blood** is used rather than **death** in order to bring this teaching concerning our Lord, and the way in which He redeems us, into line with the whole of the teaching of the Old Testament with regard to sacrifices.*
>
> D. M. Lloyd-Jones

> *Paschal Lamb, by God appointed,*
> *   All our sins on Thee were laid;*
> *By almighty love anointed,*
> *   Thou hast full atonement made:*
> *All Thy people are forgiven*
> *   Through the virtue of Thy blood;*
> *Opened is the gate of heaven;*
> *   Peace is made 'twixt man and God.*
>
> John Bakewell

NOTES

The Ten Commandments

WHEN we think of the Law of God, we normally think of it as it is found in the Ten Commandments. These were given by God to Moses after the Israelites had left Egypt and were on their way to the Promised Land. God's right to give such laws is contained in the words of verse 2. It is customary to speak of the two tables of the law.

The first table

This concerns man's duty to God. It consists of the first four commandments (vv.3-11). Here we are reminded that the Lord alone is to be our God (v.3); we are forbidden to make or worship any idols (v.4)—notice the punishment that follows the breaking of this commandment; God's name is to be regarded with the utmost reverence (v.7), and the Sabbath day is to be strictly observed (v.8). With regard to this fourth commandment, the New Testament alters the day from the seventh to the first, but the duty of remembering the day remains.

The second table

This concerns man's duty to his fellows (vv.12-17), a duty which always comes second to his duty toward God. Here we find numbered our responsibilities as members of families and members of society. Our Lord shows that this second table applies not only to our acts but to our thoughts (Matthew 5:21-28), so the spirit in which we approach the commandments is at least as important as our performance of them.

The purpose of the Law

Some people have thought that the way to become a Christian, and thus the way to heaven, is to 'keep the Ten

Commandments'. This is impossible, however, since God requires absolute perfection (Galatians 3:10), and the only One to have achieved this standard is the Son of God Himself. Then, instead of keeping the commandments, it is suggested that God will receive us if we *try* to keep them, and do our best. But this is open to the same objection. Why, then, were the Ten Commandments given?

1. To show us the holiness of God. The demands of the commandments reflect the character of God.

2. To show us, by the fact that we continually break them, how sinful we are, how short we fall of pleasing God, and how deserving we are of His condemnation.

3. To show us that we must seek salvation elsewhere than in the Law. The commandments point us to the Lord Jesus Christ as our only hope (Galatians 3:24).

All this does not mean that the Christian can forget the Ten Commandments. After a person becomes a Christian, he finds in them the pathway along which God requires him to walk.

NOTES

The New Covenant

'JEREMIAH is in prison, famine and pestilence rage in the city, and the Babylonian army is battering against the wall of Jerusalem.' This is how one writer describes the plight of the prophet and of the people. Yet with the darkness of judgment overhanging the scene, God lightens the whole picture with comfort and promise. Jeremiah may be known as 'the weeping prophet', but in this chapter is found only that which pleases. All the prospects that are held out to God's people reach their climax in the words regarding the new covenant (vv.31-34), one of the most remarkable passages not only in the prophecy but in the whole of the Old Testament.

The covenant

This was a solemn agreement which the Lord made with Abraham and his descendants, whereby He became their God and they became His people. There are many instances of the covenant in the Old Testament. Look up Exodus 24 as particularly helpful here. The covenant brought the Israelites into a special relationship with the Lord that no other nation enjoyed.

'The covenant I made'

The old covenant, established through Moses on the journey from Egypt (v.32), had one great limitation. This was not the fault of the covenant, or of its Author, who was God. The limitation arose because the people's nature was sinful, and therefore they could not keep the terms laid down by God in the covenant. It was a covenant imposed upon the people from outside themselves, and although God required them to keep it, they broke it.

'The covenant that I will make'

The new covenant that God promises to make with His people has this great difference from the old covenant. In that, obedience was pressed upon men from outside: in this, obedience rises from within themselves. This is because the terms of the new covenant are put in the people's minds, and written upon their hearts. They now *want* to keep the covenant, because they know and love the Lord and delight to experience His forgiveness. They have received a new nature.

The scope of this new covenant extends far beyond the Israelites. The Lord Jesus Christ came to establish the new agreement (Hebrews 8:6-13), which places all His redeemed people into a relationship with God that is not only unique but also eternal. It is a covenant sealed in Christ's blood. After Calvary all who believe in Christ may claim the benefits of the covenant.

NOTES

Lost and Found

THREE parables are brought before us in this chapter: the Lost Sheep, the Lost Coin, and the Lost Son. Jesus tells these parables in answer to the criticism of the Pharisees, 'This man welcomes sinners' (v.2). Praise God, Jesus does welcome sinners. To the Pharisees this was a ground for criticism: to us it is our only hope of salvation, for without it we are lost— separated from God by our sin.

Lost naturally—like the sheep
Sheep are always wandering away from the shepherd. Men are no different: 'We all, like sheep, have gone astray, each of us has turned to his own way' (Isaiah 53:6). This is our natural state, for we are born with a nature that rebels against God. It is true that a person's environment and background can be a contributory factor in his becoming a criminal and breaking the laws of society, but man breaks the laws of God naturally. We are not sinners because we sin, but we sin *because we are sinners*. That is to say, it is not what we *do* that makes us sinners: what causes us to sin is the fact that we are sinners *by nature*. This is very clearly taught in the Bible, but people do not like it and find it hard to accept.

Lost helplessly—like the coin
Here is something which is even more difficult for proud man to accept. Not only are we lost naturally, but we are also lost helplessly. What could the coin do when it was lost? Nothing. Man is dead in sin; left to himself, there is nothing he can do about it. Man is helpless in the grip of sin, and unless God takes the initiative and comes seeking sinners, he will always be lost.

If man is lost naturally and helplessly, can he be blamed? The third parable shows us that man is

Lost wilfully—like the son

Man is responsible because he chooses to be away from the love and care of the heavenly Father. His sinfulness is a wilful, deliberate, conscious act.

Here then is the picture of the sinner Jesus receives: lost and, like the sheep, too dull to know it; lost and, like the coin, helpless; lost and, like the son, wasting his life. Yet Jesus loves sinners and comes to seek and save the lost. Why are you a Christian? Is it not that Jesus found you and brought you to God? Not only does Jesus save, but He delights to save. Each parable ends with rejoicing. There is every encouragement for sinners to seek God, because He is seeking them.

While you are yet a great way off, your Father will outstrip the wind, and come, and meet you, and fall upon your neck and kiss you with kisses of reconciliation. This shall be your portion if you will trust the Lord Jesus Christ.

C. H. Spurgeon

NOTES

The Time Chosen

OVER the next five days we shall be considering the events of the last week of Christ's life. Luke takes 6 chapters out of 24 to describe just seven days in the life of Jesus; similarly, Matthew takes 8 chapters out of 28, Mark 6 out of 16, and John 10 out of 21. The importance of that last week from Palm Sunday to Easter Day cannot be overestimated. We read in several places, 'his time had not yet come' (John 7:30; 8:20). The time referred to was the time fixed by the sovereign God for His Son to die as our sin-bearer. It was a time fixed before the creation of the world (Revelation 13:8), and now that time had come (John 13:1).

The time
Very deliberately Jesus plans to die. The time is to be the Passover, that great feast of the Jews commemorating their deliverance from slavery in Egypt (Exodus 12). At the beginning of the Passover celebrations the Saviour enters Jerusalem in triumph. The Jewish authorities, although for a long time they had wanted to kill Jesus, would not have chosen to do so at the time of the Passover. But this was God's time, for Jesus is 'our Passover' (1 Corinthians 5:7), the Lamb who takes away our sins (John 1:29). By entering Jerusalem in triumph, Jesus deliberately

forces the members of the Sanhedrin to change their timetable so that it will harmonize with His (and the Father's) timetable. William Hendriksen

The entry
The mode of entry was a direct fulfilment of the Messianic prophecy of Zechariah 9:9—'See, your king comes to you,

righteous and having salvation, gentle and riding on a donkey, on a colt, the foal of a donkey.' The crowd quickly recognized this and shouted out another Messianic prophecy (v.38), which comes from Psalm 118:26.

This passage shows us very clearly that Jesus was in control. Not for a single moment during that last week did He lose control of the situation. He came to give His life a ransom for many; He chose the place and the time. The cross was no unforeseen tragedy, but the will of the sovereign God. It was all planned, all conceived in the heart and mind of our heavenly Father.

NOTES

The Last Supper

AS we read the account of the Last Supper, what strikes us immediately is the utter simplicity of it. Here we find no pomp or ceremony, no expression of deep, veiled, hidden, mystical truths: just thirteen men gathered round a simple table in what was probably a rather bare room. Yet its simplicity is its glory. We do well to keep this steadily in view. It is right to be suspicious of a communion service that loses this basic simplicity; the less mystery and obscurity we attach to it, the better it will be for our souls.

Remember

The principal object of the supper is to remind Christians of the Saviour's death for sinners. Jesus makes this clear by telling the disciples distinctly that they were to do this 'in remembrance of me' (v.19). The Lord's Table is a place not of sacrifice but of remembrance. The bread reminds us of Christ's body broken on the cross. The wine is intended to remind us of the precious blood shed to atone for our sin. The two emblems of bread and wine are intended to preach Christ crucified for us. They are a visible sermon appealing to the believer's senses, and teaching the foundational truth of the gospel, that Jesus died for sinners.

'For you'

How can we prevent the Lord's Table from becoming merely a habit, an empty meaningless ceremony? The answer is, that we are called upon to remember not just a historical event (though the death of Jesus was that), but something that has become our personal experience. This is beautifully brought out in the two words '*for you*' (vv.19,20).

The death of Jesus involves us directly and personally. It is 'for you'. On the cross Jesus was doing something for you which, if He had not done, would never have been done, and could never have been done. What Jesus did was unique. He died for you, to bring you into a new covenant relationship with God.

The new system that Jesus had established meant the forgiveness of men's sins. Men are not left to accomplish their own salvation. His blood avails to put them in right relationship to God. The new covenant is one that men may enter with assurance.   Leon Morris

This is what we remember when we come to the Lord's Table. We come in humility, with a deep sense of our sin; yet we come with joy and thanksgiving, because of the assurance that Jesus has dealt with our sin once and for all.

NOTES

Judas and Peter

WE have in this chapter the sad events of the betrayal by Judas and the denial by Peter. Two of the apostles, who had been so close to Jesus for three years, commit these terrible sins. It would seem that the ministry of Jesus had been a failure. But no, once again we see Jesus in control of the situation. He knew what Judas was doing (v.21), and He knew what Peter would do (v.34). Nothing takes Him by surprise. This in no way excuses Judas or Peter, because we are all responsible for our own sins.

Judas

'Then Satan entered Judas' (v.3; see also John 6:70,71 and John 13:26,27). This does not mean that Judas was the innocent victim of Satan. Rather it points to the fact that this apostle had never fully responded in his heart to the love of Christ. He was not a true believer. There was evidence of this long before the betrayal (John 12:4-6). Judas was fully responsible. He took the initiative and went to the priests (v.4); he took money for his betrayal (v.5); he planned and schemed for the right opportunity (v.6); he ignored the warning of Jesus (vv.21,22).

Even later (Matthew 27:3-5), when Judas realized what a terrible thing he had done, there was no repentance, only remorse. His remorse drove him not to Christ to ask forgiveness, but to suicide. 'Godly sorrow brings repentance that leads to salvation and leaves no regret, but worldly sorrow brings death' (2 Corinthians 7:10).

Peter

Satan was also involved in Peter's failure (v.31). Note the wording and see that Satan has no power to enter Peter as he did Judas. This is because Peter is a true child of God. Satan can bring all sorts of trials to the Christian, and can tempt him to sin, but he has no power to *compel* the believer to sin. The Christian is protected by the prayers of the Saviour (v.32). It is this ministry of Christ, not our strong will-power, that keeps our faith from failing completely.

If we trust our own strength, as Peter was prone to do (v.33), we will fail. Jesus knew this (v.34), and soon Peter did (v.61). Note his reactions to his sin (v.62). The reason why he wept bitterly was because he loved Jesus and hated his own sin. Even when denying Christ, he could not take his eyes off Him. Read again verse 61.

The look of Jesus would have been wasted on Peter if it had not been that Peter was looking at Jesus.

Campbell Morgan

Jesus knows our hearts, and sees true repentance, and always responds with forgiveness and love. This is hinted at in verse 32, and fulfilled in John 21:15-19.

NOTES

The Cross

THERE is much in this chapter that you need to read carefully and ponder on, but we shall confine these comments to the reaction of the crowd and the two criminals crucified with Jesus. The cross is the place where God deals once and for all with our sin. From the cross comes the request of Jesus, 'Father, forgive them' (v.34). How do men react to this great demonstration of love and mercy? Man's reaction down through the centuries is clearly mirrored in the reaction of these two criminals and the crowd looking on.

Salvation rejected

Those who rejected salvation in this passage have a common bond: it is the IF of doubt. Notice that the rulers (v.35), the soldiers (v.37), and the criminal (v.39), all expressed doubt at the claims of Jesus to be the Saviour. They were spiritually blind. There had been plenty of proof of Christ's claims, but they did not believe. This shows us how terrible is the grip of sin on the human heart and mind. Men reject salvation because sin blinds them to their own need, and to the beauty and glory of Jesus.

Salvation received

One man at least, at Calvary, saw and believed. Follow his steps of repentance.

Fear of God (v.40). Proverbs 9:10 says, 'The fear of the Lord is the beginning of wisdom.' It is also the beginning of repentance, as we realize that we are answerable to a holy God who will in no wise tolerate sin. It is an awareness that God means what He says, and that He is to be taken seriously. This leads to:

Confession of sin (v.41). When we see the holiness of God, then we see our own sinfulness. How hard it seems to be for most people to say, 'I am a sinner'! But without this confession there is no salvation.

Recognition of who Jesus is (v.41). 'This man has done nothing wrong', he says. He is not like us; we are sinners and deserve death, but He is holy and sinless. Notice that there are no 'ifs' here, but only faith in the goodness and uniqueness of Jesus. He knows, too, that Jesus is the King (v.42).

Prayer for mercy (v.42). This man was a criminal, and was therefore being crucified by Rome; at the same time he was a sinner, and was therefore under the condemnation of God. Now, freely acknowledging that he deserves nothing, he throws himself upon the mercy of Jesus. All he asks is to be remembered, but to be remembered by Jesus is enough.

Saved (v.43). In the morning the man was a condemned criminal, by the afternoon he was a redeemed sinner, by the evening he was a glorified saint! Such is the greatness of the love and mercy of God!

NOTES

The Road to Emmaus

LUKE tells us in verses 1-12 of the fact of the resurrection, but he has not yet reported any of the appearances of the risen Christ. He now does so with this most beautiful account of the living Christ drawing near to Cleopas and his friend on the road to Emmaus. These two previously unknown disciples obviously loved Jesus very much. They were very sad as they walked the seven miles from Jerusalem to their home in Emmaus. It was the evening of Easter Sunday. They knew all the facts of the crucifixion and they were downcast. The death of Jesus had shattered their cherished hopes that He was the long-promised Messiah (v.21).

They had heard rumours of the resurrection (vv.22,23), but they themselves did not believe it. It was while they were in this condition of sadness, disappointment and doubt that Jesus came to them. It would have been very easy for Jesus in a brief moment to have changed their whole disposition by simply revealing Himself to them. Instead they are 'kept from recognising him' (v.16), and for the whole of the journey of perhaps two hours they are in the presence of the risen Christ and do not know it.

'In all the Scriptures'

Why did Jesus do this? The answer is that He wanted them to see from the Scriptures (vv.25-27) that everything that had happened was in the plan and will of God. All the events that made them so downcast were necessary for man's salvation. Christ had to die; He had to suffer and bear our sin. Jesus showed them all this from the Old Testament—from 'Moses and all the Prophets'. Perhaps some of the passages mentioned were Genesis 3:15, Exodus 12:13, Numbers 21:9, Isaiah 53, Zechariah 3:1-10. .

When Jesus eventually made Himself known to them and they grasped the glorious truth of the resurrection, note their first words in verse 32. Their hearts had been 'burning' within them—that is, their depression was being replaced with excitement and anticipation—even before they recognized Jesus. It was the opening of the Scriptures that accomplished that. Not only did they see the risen Christ, but they *understood from Scripture* the full significance and glory of the cross and resurrection.

The place of Scripture in the Christian's life must be supreme. So many problems and so much heartache could be avoided if we were not so foolish and so slow of heart to believe *all* the Word of God.

NOTES

God's Last Word

THE letter to the Hebrews was written to Jews who had been converted to Christianity. Thus the writer is concerned to show not merely that Christianity grew out of Judaism, but that it is immensely superior to it. One of the ways in which he does this is by concentrating the attention of his readers upon the Lord Jesus Christ. In this chapter two truths concerning our Lord are set before us, as the author begins his mammoth task.

Who Christ is (vv.1-3)
In the Old Testament we find God's way of revealing Himself to His people. This was normally done through the words and activities of the prophets. But in Christ we have God speaking not through works or words but through a Person—His own Son. We are then led to wonder at the excellence of this Man.

Six things are said here of Christ. The splendour and glory of God abide completely in the Son, who is the exact resemblance of His Father; through Him the worlds were created; by His word all things are kept in being; He is the One to whom everything belongs; it is by Him and His sacrifice on the cross that we are washed from our sins; now His work on earth is ended and He has taken His royal seat in heaven. Could anything more perfectly describe the majesty of this Person?

Greater than the angels (vv.4-14)
Angels were prominent in the revelation of the Old Testament (Galatians 3:19; Hebrews 2:2). The superiority of the New Testament is demonstrated by the way Christ is better and greater than the angels. The contrast between Christ and

angels is shown by a series of quotations from the Old Testament. Of the seven passages produced one speaks of the angels as servants, and the others refer to Christ's relationship as Son to the Father, to His kingship, to His work as Creator and to His ultimate triumph. The only verse which speaks of Christ and the angels together requires them to worship Him; so far are they beneath Him.

While Christ is the One who has won salvation for His people, verse 14 reminds us that the angels serve the interests of the Saviour and the saved. So that although they are clearly inferior to Christ, they are not hostile or indifferent to Him, and we are greatly indebted to them.

The God who spoke to the fathers, now speaks to us. The God who spoke in old time, now speaks in these last days. The God who spoke by His prophets, now speaks by His Son.   John Brown

NOTES

Let Us Go On

TWO notes heard constantly through the letter to the Hebrews are sounded here. They are warning and encouragement.

First principles (vv.1-3)
There are certain matters to do with the gospel over which Christians have always differed, and still do. They are questions of secondary importance. There are other matters of fundamental importance, and what the opening verses of this chapter strongly indicate is that these truths must be believed and firmly held. They are like the foundations of a building; they must be secure, otherwise what is built on them will soon topple. But foundations do not need to be relaid. Thus the author says in effect, 'Let us build on these truths.' Six such truths are mentioned here.

A warning (vv.4-12)
Some people come very near to being Christian without really ever having been born again. So closely do they resemble true believers that it is often difficult, if not impossible, to tell the difference. They appear to have been under the influence of the Holy Spirit, to have partaken of the benefits held out by the Word of God, and to have been affected by the power of God. Yet they fall away, and when they do, the greatness of their crime is such that repentance is not simply improbable; it is impossible. These people must not rely upon the advantages they have shared with Christians, such as, for example, hearing the gospel; in itself that does nothing. Rain may fall on two fields; yet the one may prove fruitful, the other worthless.

In spite of this warning, the writer expresses confidence that his readers have escaped this particular snare.

An encouragement (vv.13-20)

God's promises are bound to be fulfilled. The experience of Abraham after hearing God's word (Genesis 22:16-18) is an example of this. There God made a promise accompanied by an oath, which has been fulfilled in Abraham's natural descendants (Jews) and spiritual descendants (Christians). But the promise also concerned Christ as Abraham's offspring, and this was confirmed by an oath in Psalm 110:4. This promise too has been fulfilled. And since our hope is in Christ, and this hope itself secures us, like an anchor, to heaven, we need have no fears whatever. Our great Melchizedek and High Priest, Jesus the Son of God, is a constant source of comfort and encouragement to us. Let us persevere, trusting and believing in Him.

There is urgent need that Christians in this backward and slothful condition should stir themselves to active advance towards maturity . . . The one safeguard against slipping back and falling out is to go forward. Alan M. Stibbs

NOTES

The New Takes Over the Old

THIS is an important chapter because it demonstrates the link between the Old Testament and the New. It also reveals how the promise of the Old is fulfilled in the New. It does this by contrasting Aaron and his descendants, who were the priests, with the Lord Jesus Christ, our great High Priest.

The Old Testament shadows
The worship of the Old Testament people of God centred in the Tabernacle (which later gave way to a more permanent structure, the Temple). Verses 1-10 remind us of the articles of furniture and ceremonies associated with the services of the Tabernacle. The furnishings were costly and the rituals elaborate; but, for all that, men and women could not be right with, and acceptable to, God (v.9). The reason for this was that so much of the service consisted in eating, drinking and washing, all to do with the body, but failing completely to affect the conscience. God's concern is not so much with the outward appearance. He looks on the heart (1 Samuel 16:7).

Without question, the most important feature of these ancient ceremonies was that of the sacrifice of animals. That is why this passage mentions blood so often (vv.7,12,13, 18,19, etc.).

The New Testament realities
Notice two important verses, 11 and 24. See the emphasis they lay on our Lord. They begin 'When Christ . . .' and 'For Christ . . .' In this way the writer of the letter shows how Jesus surpasses and perfects all that Aaron stood for. To the Son of

God and His work, words like 'greater', 'more perfect' (v.11), 'how much more' (v.14), 'better' (v.23) are applied.

Many points of contrast are suggested here. Consider especially the following:

The priests offered the blood of animals (v.13): Christ offered His own (vv.14,26).

The high priest entered the most Holy Place in the Tabernacle (v.7): Christ entered into heaven (v.24).

The priests dealt only in 'patterns', representations, symbols (v.23): Christ goes beyond these to the true and the real (v.24).

The high priests knew no rest from their labours, their service was constantly repeated, and therefore incomplete: Christ's sacrifice was complete and final (v.26).

It must be remembered that this chapter does not set out to show how God 'tried' the Old Testament method, and then, when it failed, sent Christ instead. The Old Testament sacrifices accomplished admirably what they were intended to do, which was to point to Him who alone could 'bear the sins of many'.

NOTES

God's Portrait Gallery

'HAVE faith in God', said Jesus on one occasion. Faith in Christ Himself is the key that unlocks all the treasures of the gospel to us. The first verse of this chapter gives us a definition of faith. Where better to find such a definition of one of the greatest words in the Bible than in the Bible itself? Verse 3 gives us an example of how faith is to be applied by us. It is not our scientific discoveries, or our reason, that enable us to understand the beginning of things, but faith. The remainder of this famous chapter is taken up with examples of people in the Old Testament who exercised faith. They form (12:1) a 'great cloud of witnesses'. The same faith is to be shown by these Hebrew Christians. Let them take heart from their ancestors. Look at the people in this list, and notice the following.

Where faith is found

It is found in all sorts of people, the great and famous, like Abraham and Moses, but also the little-known, like Barak. It is demonstrated by women as well as men; it is seen in Gentiles as well as Jews; it is seen in common people as well as royal, among the secular as well as the religious. Here it is in an upright moral person: there it is in someone of extremely doubtful reputation. Faith is not the preserve of a particular type of people. It flourishes in those of every class and kind. Look at the Christians you know and consider their differing circumstances. Faith is found everywhere.

What faith inspires

Faith accounts for astonishing facts and behaviour. It enables us to worship God and to please Him; it stood Noah in good stead when building the ark seemed unreasonable; it upholds those who dare for God. It leads to unquestioning obedience to divine commands. Men give up what they might be expected to grasp and cherish; they 'see' the invisible. Sufferings of the most dreadful kind are patiently borne through faith. Nothing is impossible to those who believe.

How faith is rewarded
Men of faith are often great losers in terms of this world's advantages, but their reward is no less satisfying or certain for that. They look to the future all the time. On this earth they are not at home; their eyes, however, are fixed on a 'city with foundations', 'a better country'. They are persuaded that God will honour their faith.

Let this hymn in praise of faith be a continual exhortation to us.

What should we do if we had not faith and hope to lean on, and if our mind did not emerge amidst the darkness above the world by the shining of the Word and Spirit of God?
John Calvin

NOTES

The Call of God

SAMUEL was a young boy growing up in a period of serious spiritual declension. The priests were corrupt (2:12-17). Eli was a good man but very weak, and he failed to discipline his sons (3:13). The result was, 'the word of the Lord was rare' (v.1). At this time the Lord chose and called young Samuel to be a prophet to the nation. The long-term implications and consequences of this call were enormous, but in today's reading just think of the call itself.

The call of God mistaken

According to the Jewish historian Josephus, Samuel was now about 12 years old. By this age he was familiar with the worship and procedure of the Temple, having lived in and around the great centre of worship almost all his life; but he 'did not yet know the Lord' (v.7). Familiarity with worship and church services do not guarantee that we know the Lord. Something more is needed. We must have a personal experience of the living God, and this is always preceded by God calling us to Himself.

God called Samuel; it was a very clear call, but he thought it came from Eli. How often do we fail to recognize God's call, putting it down to the words of a preacher, or a friend's influence, or our own emotion! Thank God for His infinite patience with us! Three times He called Samuel.

The call of God answered

Eli realizes what is happening (vv.8,9) and instructs Samuel accordingly. For all his faults, the old priest was still able to recognize the work of God. It is strange, but true, that often others can see the Lord dealing with us before we ourselves are aware of it.

Samuel now understands and waits for God to speak again. When the Lord comes (v.10), the young boy answers 'Speak, for your servant is listening.' This is more than just a repetition of Eli's words (v.9). For the first time Samuel is conscious of the presence of Almighty God. He wants to hear and obey the Word of God; he has begun a new and sweet communion with the Lord, which is to continue for the rest of his life.

The emergence of such spiritual character right from the time that he first responded to God is a rebuke to our own attitude. In our Christian work and witness we do not seem to look for this kind of conversion and consecration . . . this is what we want to see in the context of the preaching of the gospel and the call to discipleship, 'Speak, Lord, for thy servant heareth.'   George Philip

NOTES

A Challenge

THE armies of those bitter enemies, the Philistines and the Israelites, faced each other and made ready for battle. This had happened on many occasions, but this time there was a difference. The Philistines had a champion named Goliath, and they were so confident that no one could defeat him that they were prepared to trust everything to him (v.9).

The challenger seemed invincible (vv.8-11)

Over nine feet tall, Goliath must have been a fearsome sight (vv.4-7). His challenge for single combat to settle the battle seemed unanswerable, and the Philistines, trusting in the size and strength of their champion, had no doubt of victory. Who could possibly beat this giant? The Israelites, sharing their opinion, were panic-stricken (v.11). The people of God had forgotten the power the Lord their God could give them, and they cowered before a man.

The Goliaths of this present day still come shouting their challenges to us, confident in their strength and power. Whilst the challenges presented to a Christian today are no doubt great, do you think they are invincible?

The resources seemed inadequate

No one was willing to meet the challenge: not King Saul, who had known many great victories previously (chapter 11); not Jonathan, who had already had a remarkable victory over the Philistines (chapter 14). They all thought they were inadequate to meet Goliath, and had no heart for the battle.

David was the only one willing to fight. Why? Read verses 34-37. He had already proved that God's resources were more than adequate, and he was ready to trust the Lord again. Do you think the Christian's resources are inadequate to meet today's challenges? Listen then to David in verses 45-47.

The result seemed inevitable

No one gave David a hope of victory. Not even his brother Eliab (v.28), nor the king (v.33), and certainly not Goliath (v.44). So often Christians are put off by difficulties and just accept what appears to be inevitable; but there is nothing that cannot be changed by a faith like David's. The only thing that is really inevitable is the ultimate triumph of God. When you start thinking that defeat cannot be helped, remember David and Goliath. Goliath seemed to have every advantage—size, strength, experience and weapons. But David went in the name of the Lord, and victory was his. Never forget that 'the battle is the Lord's' (v.47). The giants that may be challenging your Christian life—some secret sin, the fear of witnessing, an inability to pray—will all fall when your sole trust is in the Lord's strength (Psalm 31:14-16; Psalm 56:9-11).

NOTES

Asa—Trusting God

ASA was one of the few good kings that either Israel or Judah had. Most were ungodly men who, by example and command, led the people away from God to idols. Asa was different, as is evident from verses 2-5. As soon as he became king he went into battle, not against the traditional enemies (foreign nations), but against the real enemy (sin). Verses 3-5 describe a very real battle, and it was one in which God gave Asa victory. The result was that for several years the land enjoyed peace and rest. That was very unusual at the time, and Asa gladly acknowledged that it was 'because we have sought the Lord our God' (v.7). When a nation, or a church, or an individual, seeks to give God His proper and rightful place, then the Lord honours it.

The fight

There is to be no peace treaty with sin. The Christian must fight it, and that fight takes place first and foremost in his own life. It is then that the peace of God, and the rest which Christ alone gives, are gloriously and wonderfully experienced. But the fact that the child of God enjoys this peace and rest does not mean that he is now immune to external pressures. Asa knew peace for ten years; then Zerah came against him with a vast army (v.9). Why did this happen? If the Lord had given peace for ten years, why did He not give it for another ten? Was it that Asa had sinned and this was God's punishment? There are no grounds for saying that.

God allowed the enemy to come, not as a punishment but as an encouragement. In times of trouble we learn more of God's care and love for us, and we discover an even deeper rest and peace as we are thrown entirely upon the mercy of God. Asa was confronted with an enemy far too strong for him, but instead of giving way to panic or despair, he prays. We all need to learn this lesson well.

The prayer

'Asa called to the Lord his God' (v.11). What a lesson this is for us! Is not Asa's God *our* God? In times of extreme trouble it is not men we need, or money, or schemes. We need God. Read Psalm 20:5-7.

Notice how Asa prayed:

His confidence is in the power of God—*'there is no-one like you'*. Our God is able.

His request is simple—*'Help us'*. God loves to hear His people ask for help.

His trust is in the Lord—*'we rely on you'*. This is the only way to face the enemy. We are not to rely on our knowledge, our ability, our strength, but solely on the Lord.

His hope is in the *name* of God (compare this with David facing Goliath in 1 Samuel 17:45), and in the fact that He is *'our* God'.

Such confidence and faith are never misplaced. We see the Lord answering prayer in verse 12. Does not this give you a sense of excitement? Is it not a privilege to be in the battle? 'The battle is the Lord's' (1 Samuel 17:47).

NOTES

98

Asa—Ignoring God

YESTERDAY we saw Asa exercising remarkable faith and trust in God: today's chapter takes place twenty-six years later, and we see a very different Asa now. Here we have a man who relies on men, not God (v.7), and who seeks help from men, not God (v.12). Instead of taking delight in praying to God, he now gets angry when God speaks to him (v.10).

How can a man change so much?

Is this Asa? Is this he whose heart was perfect with the Lord his God all his days? Well, let him that thinketh he stands, take heed lest he fall. A wise man! and yet in a rage! A good man! and yet impatient of reproof, and cannot bear to be told of his faults! Lord, what is man when God leaves him to himself?
Matthew Henry

Mistakes

It is easy for us to see all the mistakes Asa made. But why could *he* not see them? What Hanani said to him in verses 7 and 8 was so obvious, yet not only could Asa not see it himself, but he was angry when told about it. Even more importantly, perhaps, for the remaining five years of his life he never learned the lesson of this failure.

Prosperity

Perhaps the answer is that years of prosperity and comfort (15:19) had taken the spiritual edge off Asa's life. For years he had had things easy, and there had been no great crisis forcing him to turn to God. The spiritual triumphs of former years became but a memory. Somewhere along the way Asa must have lost daily, personal communion with God.

If you are just starting out on the Christian life, learn in the early days that yesterday's blessing will not meet today's problems. We must have a fresh, daily experience of God. This is why daily Bible reading and prayer are so crucial. A stale Christian experience provides fertile ground for the devil to sow seeds of sin.

The church in Laodicea (Rev. 3:14-22) has stood for nineteen hundred years as a serious warning to the whole church of Christ to be most watchful when no enemy is in sight and to remain poor in spirit when earthly wealth increases.   A. W. Tozer

One last comment: do not think that verse 12 is teaching us not to see the doctor when we are ill. Read the verse carefully, and you will see that the criticism is not that he went to the physicians, but that he completely ignored the Lord. We thank God for hospitals, doctors and medicines, and we pray that the Lord will use them to maintain our health and the health of those fortunate enough to have their services.

NOTES

Dealing with Deceit

CHRISTIANITY has always been confronted with errors. Paul had to alert the early church to certain dangers. Similarly today we need to be on our guard, sometimes against the same kind of perils. We need to be watchful on account of false teaching that some are concerned to spread in the name of Jesus Christ. In Colosse certain people were leading the Christians astray, not by a heresy that could at once be recognized as obviously anti-Christian, but by a subtle emphasis on the need for added knowledge and enlightenment. Here Paul counsels his friends in the church as to how to deal with this deception.

Christ alone sufficient (vv.6-15)
Christians do not need any 'extra' philosophy. Christ Himself is all the wisdom and knowledge they require. Perhaps what these believers at Colosse need (and what we need today?) is to understand what happened to them when they became Christians. They are to go on as they began, walking by faith (v.6), and not being misled by human worldly teachings that do not have the authority of Christ (v.8). Christ *is* God, and therefore all authority rightly belongs to Him (v.9). When they were baptized, that was an indication that they had been buried with Christ, that they had finished with the principles and rules of men, and that they had been raised to a new life (v.12). Sin's authority in their lives was cancelled by the death of the Lord Jesus on the cross. There, it was openly robbed of its power over believers.

Freedom from tradition (vv.16-23)
Because they are free, and own only Christ as their Lord, they need not bow to the regulations imposed on them from the

outside. They need not observe this particular occasion, or remember that particular festival. These are like shadows. Where there is a shadow there is a reality. Before we knew Christ, we needed these lesser things, but now we have found Christ, the reality, we finish with the shadows. If we go back to them, then we are prisoners to them. People who take us away from the freedom we have in Christ are to be avoided, however impressive their claims and qualifications may be.

Death with Christ, the experience of every Christian, is death to the principles according to which we lived our former lives. Learn early in your Christian experience to distinguish between the old way of living your life, and the new. For the latter, Christ is all you need.

> *Get them* [the people] *well to heaven, and they will have knowledge enough . . . Many other things are desirable to be known; but this must be known.* Richard Baxter

NOTES

God's People

BY believing in the Lord Jesus Christ we become Christians. But the matter does not rest there. We must go on, develop, grow. This we do mainly by means of spiritual food—the Word of God (v.2).

Belonging to God (vv.4-10)
The Lord Jesus is described as a 'Stone'. For this understanding Peter goes back into the Old Testament. There he finds reference to the Stone being chosen. Christ was appointed by His Father as the One on whom the salvation of His people rests. All who rest on Him are God's. However, Peter sees in the Old Testament that there are some who turn away from this Stone. They reject Him. This is mainly a reference to the religious leaders of the Jews. They ought to have seen the worth of this Stone, but instead of that they discarded it. Still using the figure of a stone, although not now a stone in building, Peter shows his readers that there are some who trip over this Stone (v.8). And so, rather than being for their benefit, it brings about their downfall. So men's response to Christ determines whether they go to heaven or to hell. If men are rightly related to the Stone, the Lord Jesus, then they enjoy all the privileges of being God's people (v.9).

Suffering for Christ (vv.11-20)
Peter now encourages the Christians on their way. They and we are to live so as to give no offence whatever to those who do not receive our message. He gives practical examples of what this will involve. Everyone must be submissive to the government. Christians should be the very last people to be disobedient to authority.

As far as servants are concerned they must respect their

masters. It does not matter whether their employers are unjust or unkind. Indeed, to suffer unjustly is a remarkable opportunity of glorifying God. Enduring suffering when we deserve it is no credit. But if we take patiently punishment wrongly administered, we reflect honour upon God. Peter points to the example of Christ's patience in suffering. But Peter cannot remain long on the subject of Christ's sufferings merely as an example. He must move on to the deeper significance of His enduring on the cross in our place (vv.21-25). Once more He turns to the Old Testament Scriptures to drive home his lesson. See how important to Peter, and to other writers of the New Testament, was the prophecy of Isaiah (v.22 being a quote from Isaiah 53:9).

Expect to be reviled and buffeted, misunderstood and misrepresented, cast out and crucified as He was. The sheep cannot expect to fare better than the Shepherd.

F. B. Meyer

NOTES

A New Direction

THE difference between the lives we lived as non-Christians and those we live now as Christians ought to be crystal clear. As followers of Christ we have finished with pursuing evil, sinful desires. Now our time is spent in pleasing God.

Abuse from friends (vv.3-6)
Your past life was taken up with ungodly living—and you have spent enough time in that kind of behaviour. Because you are new creatures you live a new kind of life. Your friends, whose company you enjoyed in your former pleasures, will no longer understand you, and will pour their scorn upon you because of the change of direction your life has taken (v.4). But remember this: for continuing in the way of life that you have abandoned they will have to render an account (v.5).

Ruled by love (vv.7-11)
Love must direct your conduct. It must govern your attitude towards one another in practical matters such as hospitality, and in more spiritual forms of service. You deal in God's grace, God's words, God's strength, and all to His glory.

Hardship to be expected (vv.12-19)
Since Peter is writing to Christians who are in the midst of suffering, it is to be expected that he should have much to say on the subject. He returns to the question frequently in the course of the letter. Here he introduces a warning. Christians are not to be surprised when they suffer. Rather, they are to see the path they have chosen as being marked by suffering for the sake of Christ.

It is the way the Master went;
Should not the servant tread it still?

Horatius Bonar

Such suffering is to be greeted with rejoicing because it means that you have the privilege of bearing a part in our Lord's sufferings (v.13). If you rejoice in suffering for Him, think of that joy you will experience in the last day when He will be seen in glory. Only make sure that when you suffer it is not for wrongdoing, but as a Christian, for well-doing—and do not be ashamed (vv.15,16). Judgment—and therefore hardship—always begins with God's people. What dreadful fate awaits those for whom judgment is still future! And if Christians are not saved without difficulty, what hope can there possibly be for those who reject the gospel (v.18)?

Make sure that you have committed yourselves to God's safe keeping, as those who suffer not by accident but by the purpose of God.

NOTES

The Revelation of Jesus Christ

IN the midst of extreme persecution and danger, God hastens to give comfort and encouragement to His children. This is what the book of Revelation is about. To the apostle John, himself an exile on the island of Patmos (v.9), is given this glorious message of consolation to share with other suffering Christians. The seven churches in Asia (v.11) are particularly in mind.

Greetings (vv.4-8)
'Grace and peace' was a familiar greeting in the letters of the New Testament. Notice here reference to the Trinity (vv.4,5), the 'seven spirits' indicating 'the Holy Spirit in the fulness of His operations and influences in the world and in the Church' (Wm. Hendriksen). The troubled hearts of these Christians were immediately directed to the love of God and the salvation it had won by the death of Christ on the cross (v.5). To Him be all the praise! His triumph will one day be evident to everyone (v.7).

The vision of the Lord Jesus Christ (vv.9-16)
In the desolate surroundings to which he has been expelled, John is granted one of the most sublime visions ever given to man. Consider the symbolism that abounds in this description.

The *robe* and the *sash* speak of majesty and royalty. Here is One who is kingly in His appearance and in verse 5 is given the title 'the ruler of the kings of the earth'.

The *head* and *hair* give the Person a venerable appearance. Their whiteness suggests intense holiness and great age. Christ is eternal. Look up Daniel 7:9.

His *eyes* are piercing. Nothing escapes their all-seeing gaze. He knows what it is that the churches are called upon to endure.

His *feet* would tread down all the enemies that were then troubling the Christians. Let Christ's foes tremble.

When He speaks, His *voice* strikes terror in the hearts of those against whom His words are directed. It is the voice of authority. For a little while it may be silent, but beware when it is raised.

His authority is again symbolized by the sword that issues from His *mouth*. Turn to Hebrews 4:12.

His *smile* shines upon the churches—they are His. Upon them He lifts up the light of His countenance.

Christ's encouragement (vv.17-20)
The relevance of all this to the churches is seen when we realize that this Person is in the midst of the lampstands. Verse 20 supplies the key. The angels (or ministers) of the churches are in the strong right hand of Christ, and superintending all the affairs and fortunes of the churches is the great Head of the Church Himself.

NOTES

A New Leader

THE death of Moses was a heavy blow for Israel. He was the man God had used to bring them out of slavery in Egypt, and for the past forty years he had led them during their journey to the Promised Land. On many occasions they resented his leadership, yet they knew he was God's man. They had reached a point now when they needed Moses more than ever, for with hardly any experience of warfare they were about to face the seven hostile nations who lived in Canaan. It was at that precise moment that the Lord took Moses from them. 'Moses my servant is dead.' That they felt this death very keenly is obvious from Deuteronomy 34:8.

Are we not always prone to associate God's work with a man, and to think that if for some reason the man goes, the work is finished? If a pastor has been the means of great blessing to a church, and then is called by God to another church, so often God's people seem lost and confused. We have to learn that the work of God is in no way hindered by the removal of His servant, no matter how great and godly a man he has been.

God will change hands to show that whatever instrument He uses, He is not tied to any.   Matthew Henry

God's work

The Lord emphasizes over and over again in verses 2-9 that He is in control. This does not mean that the people are to sit idle while God does it all for them. Canaan is God's gift to His people, but they must fight for every inch of it. There are many battles to be fought; but the victory is assured because it is God's work. The almighty God could easily have given them a smooth and swift path to possession of the Promised

Land, but it was neither smooth nor swift. This taught them how dependent they were on the Lord.

Remember this when in your Christian life the battles seem to come thick and fast.

God's man
God took Moses away and gave the people Joshua. Joshua must have felt very inadequate, but look in verse 5 at the mighty encouragement God gave him. Here was God's chosen man, but, like all who are on the Lord's side, he must be careful to obey God's revealed word (v.7). Read verse 8, and memorize it. If you want your life to bring glory to God, this is the way—the only way.

If we would prosper as Joshua did, then we must act as he did.   A. W. Pink

NOTES

Holy, Holy, Holy!

Isaiah saw the Lord, but in a vision. In a mysterious manner the power of God came over the prophet, so that he became unconscious to the outside, external world, and yet with the inner eye saw what God revealed to him. It was thus a divinely imposed vision, one that was objective to Isaiah in that it was not the product of Isaiah's mind.

E. J. Young

What Isaiah saw was not the product of a fertile and imaginative mind, but a God-given vision. There are many lessons to be learnt from this chapter but the most important is that we increasingly appreciate something of the holiness of God.

The vision (vv.1-4)

Isaiah saw God 'seated on a throne'. This is the view we need to have of the Lord. He is not some little god waiting for our instructions, but a sovereign, mighty God, who rules and reigns over the universe. Never forget that God is still on the throne. Before this throne the angelic seraphs worship and adore the Lord with the cry, 'Holy, holy, holy is the Lord Almighty.' The holiness of God is His uniqueness, awesomeness, His moral excellence and perfection. He is so pure and without flaw that He cannot look on sin (Habakkuk 1:13). Holiness implies two things: entire freedom from all moral evil, and absolute moral perfection. This is our God. He is holy, not because He conforms to a standard; He *is* the standard. Holiness is the very beauty of God.

The holiness of God is His glory; as His grace is His riches, so holiness is His crown.   Stephen Charnock

Is this your view of God? It does not matter if you never

111

have a vision, but it is vital that you recognize what God is like. Isaiah's mind was deeply impressed with the kingly majesty of God, His holiness and purity.

The reaction (v.5)

In a sense, the prophet's reaction in verse 5 was inevitable, once he had truly seen the holiness of God. Uncleanness and unworthiness were exposed in the light of divine purity. This means that a true realization of the character of God will affect the way we draw near to God in worship. Both Moses and Joshua were told to take their shoes off because they were standing on holy ground (Exodus 3:5, Joshua 5:15). This teaches us that the hallmark of true worship is not noise and flippant familiarity, but awe, wonder, reverence, combined with a deep joy. It is the *holy* God that we worship.

> *O worship the Lord in the beauty of holiness;*
> *Bow down before Him, His glory proclaim;*
> *With gold of obedience and incense of lowliness,*
> *Kneel and adore Him, the Lord is His Name.*

John Samuel Bewley Monsell

NOTES

A Mighty God

THIS remarkable chapter vibrates throughout with the greatness, glory and might of our God. 'Here is your God!' says Isaiah (v.9). This chapter ought to be read regularly by every believer, particularly at times when we need comfort and encouragement. Isaiah's remedy at such times is to ask us, 'Do you not know? Have you not heard?' (vv.21,28). Don't you realize, he says, how great your God is?

Here is a God who is outside the barrier of time, who is not limited by the circumstances of life, but who stands over and above all these things and acts as only the mighty God can act. This chapter was written 700 years before the birth of Christ; yet verses 3-5 speak so clearly of John the Baptist (Luke 3:4-6). Even in Isaiah's time, and long before that, the Lord was planning the coming of His Son to be our Saviour. What a comfort!

So often we are overcome by such things as despair, confusion, fear and self-pity. The unfailing answer to these is to realize afresh the Person and character of our God.

Here we have the answer to:

(a) *despair* (vv.10-12). How can we despair when the sovereign Lord is with us?

(b) *confusion* (vv.13,14). We are often confused, but the Lord is omniscient, He knows everything. Read carefully verse 26. Isn't this both amazing and beautiful? Every star in the sky God knows by name. When He brings them out, not one is missing. He is never at a loss, never confused, always in complete control.

(c) *fear* (vv.21-24). Fear of the world situation and of the power of nations can be very real, but here it is all put into perspective. The Lord reigns.

(d) *self-pity* (vv.27-31). Self-pity is such a destructive force. How many times have you felt like making the complaint in verse 27? You are forsaken and disregarded, you think, and you hide in self-pity. There is no need of this. 'Do you not know? Have you not heard' about this mighty God described in verses 28-31? Christian, here is your God! Away with self-pity, and instead worship and praise the living God.

One last thought from Matthew Henry commenting on verse 31:

> *To wait upon the Lord* [NIV, 'hope in the Lord'] *means to commit ourselves to God's guidance, rely upon Him by faith and sincerely live each day according to His Word. As our work is renewed, our strength will be renewed: as the need arises, we 'shall be anointed with fresh oil', and as the day so shall our strength be. When we do these things, we will find that God's grace is always sufficient for us!*

NOTES

A Great Promise

THE opening verses of this chapter contain a great and precious promise which the Lord makes to His people: 'I will be with you.' The Christian is not immune to the problems of life. On the contrary, very often he gets more than his share because he has to cope not only with the difficulties that confront all men, but also with spiritual attacks about which the unbeliever knows nothing. In these trials he is not alone, because his God and Saviour has promised to be with him. When the waters of sorrow and the fires of affliction begin to close upon him, the Christian has the great comfort of knowing the sustaining presence and power of Almighty God.

Christians only

This promise the Lord makes to His people, and to them alone. The promise is to those of whom God says 'you are mine' (v.1). But do not all people belong to God? Is He not the Father of everyone? No, He is not. God is the Creator of all, and the Judge of all, but He is only the Father of those who are 'in Christ' (Ephesians 2:13), who have been 'adopted' into the family of God (Ephesians 1:5; 2:19). We are reminded of this special relationship in verse 1: 'I have redeemed you; I have called you by name; you are mine.' The Christian is a person who belongs to God, purchased by the blood of Christ (Acts 20:28), and he is one who is very precious to the Lord (v.4).

Claiming the promise

Read verse 2 again. Do you believe God means what He says? How then do you make the promise real in your life? There are two things you must remember:

(a) *Remember who you are.* When trials and tribulations come, remember that you belong to God, you are precious to Him, and you can therefore look for and expect His help. So often Christians forget this, and they panic and flounder like everyone else. Do you remember the story of the Israelites, redeemed out of slavery in Egypt and on their way to the Promised Land? Then they confront their first problem: Pharaoh comes after them with his army, and they cannot escape because the Red Sea bars their way. What do they do? They panic—read Exodus 14:10-12. They forget they have been redeemed; they forget all that the Lord has done for them. Moses has to rebuke them: 'Do not be afraid. Stand firm and you will see the deliverance the Lord will bring you today' (Exodus 14:13). Do not make their mistake. Remember that you are the Lord's, and therefore He will be with you.

(b) *Remember who God is.* God is almighty, and no situation is beyond His power. When you cannot cope, He can. Read 2 Corinthians 12:9,10.

Remember who God is and trust Him all the way. He will never let you down.

NOTES

Man of Sorrows

THE prophet Isaiah wrote these verses 700 years before Christ died at Calvary. Yet the description is so incredibly accurate that it sounds as if it had been written in the very shadow of the cross! It is of Jesus that the prophet is writing, and this fact alone has thrilled and warmed the hearts of Christians down the centuries. This was the chapter explained by Philip, which led to the conversion of the first African (Acts 8:26-39).

The facts

The facts of our Saviour's life are here brought before us:

His birth in obscurity and poverty— *'like a root out of dry ground'*.

His humble surroundings hid His true glory— *'no beauty or majesty'*.

He met with unbelief and opposition— *'despised and rejected'*.

He experienced unknown depths of suffering— *'a man of sorrows'*.

No one was able to convict Him of sin— *'he had done no violence . . . nor . . . any deceit'*.

He was the victim of a miscarriage of justice— *'By oppression and judgment, he was taken away.'*

In the face of all this He did not complain— *'he did not open his mouth.'*

He was put to death— *'cut off from the land of the living'*.

He was identified with criminals— *'numbered with the transgressors.'*

He was buried in a rich man's tomb—*'with the rich in his death'.*

Their meaning

Yes, the facts are all there, but we also have the meaning of the facts. Ten times the doctrine of Christ's substitutionary atonement is referred to (vv.4-6,8,11,12). He died *in the sinner's place.* 'He took up our infirmities . . . our sorrows . . . our transgressions . . . our iniquities.'

> *In my place condemned He stood;*
> *Sealed my pardon with His blood.*
>
> Philipp Paul Bliss

Jesus died, the Just for the unjust, to make atonement for our sin, and Isaiah makes it very clear that this was God's plan: 'it was the Lord's will to crush him and cause him to suffer' (v.10). Jesus was 'stricken by God' (v.4). This is exactly what Peter preached at Pentecost: all this had happened 'by God's set purpose' (Acts 2:23). The same truth is repeated in Acts 4:28—'They did what your power and will had decided beforehand should happen.'

> *The salvation that is all of God is a salvation wrought out on a cross, by a death which perfectly accorded with God's purpose.*
>
> Leon Morris

We can be absolutely sure that Christ's death on the cross is able to atone for our sins and make us acceptable to God, because this was the way God had planned to save souls. This confidence is further emphasized in the triumph of verse 12. Jesus 'bore the sin of many'. Praise God for that!

> *Hallelujah! what a Saviour!*

NOTES

False Prophets

THIS chapter shows what importance God attaches to the truth, and how strongly He is opposed to those who would deny it—the false prophets. 'I am against you, declares the Sovereign Lord' (v.8).

The people of God have always been troubled by false prophets. They were causing trouble in Old Testament times; Paul had problems with them in the New Testament era, and they are very much with us today. These men may be charming, delightful, pleasant and even sincere, but God is against them because the damage they do is horrific. This damage is twofold (v.22):

(a) *They dishearten the righteous.* They cast doubt on the truth and authority of Scripture. They deny the believer's conversion experience and destroy his assurance of salvation.

(b) *They encourage the wicked.* They teach that everyone goes to heaven, and there is no hell. They deny the necessity of being born again, and proclaim salvation by works. They lead people astray by saying '"Peace", when there is no peace' (v.10).

Whitewash (v.11)
This word, in many ways, sums up the message of the false prophets. They always by-pass the problem of man's sin and guilt before the holy God. Instead of making people aware of their true condition, they encourage them to build flimsy walls of their own self-righteousness. There must always be a nice, comfortable feeling of well-being amongst their hearers, and so an easy religion, a sentimental doctrine, is presented, with not so much as a mention of sin, or guilt, or conviction, or judgment. It is all whitewash—a covering over of gross

deficiencies; a refusal to face up to reality, and to admit that these flimsy walls men are building are totally unacceptable to Almighty God.

The trouble with whitewash is that it wears off; it has no permanence; heavy rain soon removes it (v.13). In the same way God's wrath and judgment will expose such false teaching (vv.14-16).

This problem is a very real one today, and for this reason the New Testament has a lot to say on the matter. Read Matthew 7:15-20, Galatians 1:6-9, 2 Peter 2:1-3, 1 John 4:1-3, 2 John 7-11, and Jude.

False prophets are a danger to your soul, so do not listen to their preaching, and do not read their books. How do you recognize them? The hallmark of the false prophet is that he ignores the exclusive claims of Jesus to be the only way to God; he scorns the Bible and presents his own ideas instead of the Word of God. They 'prophesy out of their own imagination' (v.2).

NOTES

The Valley of Dry Bones

EZEKIEL'S vision of the valley of dry bones is a remarkable story, but the story itself is only a vehicle to bring to us a truth from God. This is made clear in verse 11. Ezekiel, as the result of an activity of the Holy Spirit which we cannot understand (v.1), finds himself in the middle of a valley full of dead men's bones. The bones were 'very dry' (v.2)—the men had been dead a long time—and there were not just a few of them, but the valley was full.

God first asks Ezekiel a question: 'Can these bones live?' (v.3). Then He gives the prophet a command (v.4): '**Prophesy** to these bones'—that is, preach to them. They **must 'hear the** Word of the Lord.'

God used this remarkable illustration to show **the true** spiritual condition of Israel (v.11), and the same story speaks to us clearly of the spiritual state of our nation today. This is how God sees Britain—a valley of dry bones, a nation spiritually dead and with no hope. It is a frightening but accurate picture.

'Can these bones live?'

Will the people ever love and serve the Lord? To the eye of man those disjointed bones spell out despair and impossibility. Notice the prophet's answer: 'O Sovereign Lord, you alone know' (v.3). To men, even to a prophet, it is impossible, but not to a SOVEREIGN LORD. Do you believe that God can bring our unbelieving nation to Himself? Can God revive this land? Can these bones live? This is the question every Christian asks as he looks at his spiritually dead relatives, friends and neighbours.

'Prophesy to these bones'

This is God's answer to a seemingly impossible situation. Notice the command in verse 4, and the promise in verses 5 and 6. Ezekiel obeyed (v.7), and as he preached God's word to this lifeless congregation a remarkable thing happened. Divine power began to operate. The face of spiritual death began gradually to change (vv.7-10) until, under the ministry of the word of God, dry bones, dead souls came to life.

What a tremendous encouragement this is to us to tell men and women the gospel message! We serve a sovereign God to whom nothing is impossible. He saved you and He can save others. If we view only the problems and the opposition to the gospel, we will despair and do nothing; but if we see our God as almighty, sovereign and omnipotent, we will soon agree with William Carey, who said, 'Expect great things from God; attempt great things for God.'

NOTES

The Gospel of Christ

HOW completely Paul had been captured by the good news of salvation through Jesus Christ! What great confidence it had given him of its power! The letter to the Romans provides the best, clearest and lengthiest statement of the gospel in the whole of the Bible. The key to this remarkable letter is very probably found in verse 17 of this chapter —it is by faith in Christ that men are counted right with God.

The foundation of the gospel
The basis of the message is that God has done something remarkable for men and women in the Lord Jesus Christ. Christ is completely man and fully God. He was raised from the dead. To Him all men are summoned to submit themselves.

The desire created by the gospel
Paul's love for other men and women shines out brightly here, and is the direct result of the influence of the gospel. With regard to other Christians he thanks God for them, he prays for them, he longs to see them. Notice (v.12) the apostle's humility in recognizing that it is not simply a case of his having something to give to the Christians at Rome: they also have something to contribute to him. Your minister needs you and your encouragement as much as you need him and his!

As far as other men are concerned, Paul confesses himself to be a debtor. As Christians we owe it to others to share the gospel with them, whoever they are. God requires it. It is the longing that others may come to have everlasting life that drives the apostle Paul in his endeavours. Is your zeal like this?

The task confronting the gospel

The passage from verse 18 to the end of the chapter brings before us one of the most dreadful and alarming descriptions of the sinful condition of men found anywhere in Scripture.

They have turned away deliberately from the knowledge of God that He Himself has given in creation. This renders them 'without excuse'.

The decline that sets in when men reject God is frightening. *We* might prefer to pass over in silence the kind of behaviour that results; but the Bible, honest as ever, refuses to do this. It forces us to consider these offensive features and says to us, 'This is what happens when men forget God.' Men reach their lowest level when they not only practise these sins but actually commend them.

Perhaps the most solemn words in the chapter are the repeated warnings that 'God gave them over'. We dare not take God's patience and apparent indifference for granted. He allows men to pursue the course they have chosen—to their eternal grief.

This is the field to be conquered by the gospel.

We see how terrible to his posterity have been the consequences of the sin of the first man; and on the other hand, how glorious in the plan of redemption is the grace of God by His Son.   Robert Haldane

NOTES

Justification by Faith

'THE crucial and vital doctrine of "justification by faith"' is how Dr. D. M. Lloyd-Jones describes this subject. There is no more important teaching in the Bible than this, and nowhere is it set out more clearly and explicitly than in this chapter.

The righteousness of God (vv.1-8)
Paul is anxious to show how upright and faithful God is in His dealings with men. Whatever arguments men may produce in their attempts to show that God is unfair, the apostle insists that nothing can overthrow the great principle of truthfulness and justice in the way God saves sinners. Is it unjust of God to condemn us, when our wickedness sets in relief His righteousness? Are we not, by our sinfulness, setting off God's splendour more brightly, and therefore bringing Him glory? Such reasoning is unworthy and is to be condemned.

Universal sinfulness (vv.9-20)
No group of people is any better or worse than any other in God's sight. Jews and Gentiles are alike sinful. To prove this Paul turns to the Old Testament and gives a catalogue of quotations indicating clearly how ungodly and unrighteous men are. It is a truly dreadful list. Paul emphasizes that what he has to say is true of everyone. Their words, their actions, their whole attitude to God leaves them with no excuse and no escape from the judgment of God. The law that God has given provides no refuge; it is not a way of salvation, for the simple reason that no one has kept it. Indeed, what the law does is to make us aware of our sin.

Righteousness by faith (vv.21-31)

How then, can men become right with God, if the law condemns them? Remarkably there is a way, and it is the law itself that points to this way; the prophetic writings in the Old Testament also bear witness to it. It is the way of faith. Although all are deserving of the wrath of God, in His love God has sent Jesus Christ to die on the cross, to pay the penalty for our sins, and to turn away God's anger. God's justice and mercy come together in this.

In this way men are justified. This does not mean that they are made perfect, but they are counted and regarded as being so because Christ has died in their place. It is impossible for anyone to boast of his relationship with God, as though he himself had contributed anything to that relationship. To make men right with God is the work of God, and all that men do is to receive the benefits of that work by faith. This is equally true of Jews and Gentiles, and does no violence whatever to the law of God.

NOTES

The Way of Acceptance

PEACE, hope, joy—these are some of the many blessings that are enjoyed by the Christian; and he enjoys them as a result of his new relationship with God.

Peace with God (vv.1-11)
If you like, this is the first of the blessings to which we are introduced as Christians. The others flow out of this. Paul states his case clearly in verse 1: we have peace with God on account of what Christ has done for us. This must mean that before we receive Christ into our hearts, we do not have peace. And if we do not have peace with God, we must be His enemies. Look at the words Paul uses to describe those for whom Christ died—'ungodly', 'sinners', 'enemies'—in other words, people whose thinking, life and attitude were completely opposed to God. These who once were hostile to God have now 'received reconciliation' through the death of Jesus Christ on the cross. This being so, they are prepared to endure sufferings for Christ's sake, in the knowledge that through these sufferings God is continuing to work out His purpose in them.

Adam and Christ (vv.12-21)
In this somewhat difficult passage Adam and Christ are compared and contrasted. Both are heads of companies of people. Adam represents the whole company of mankind; he is the father of the human race. The Lord Jesus Christ represents all Christians. The contrast between the 'first' and the 'last' Adam is then set out in certain specific terms.

Sin, and therefore death, came into the world and dominated all men because of Adam's disobedience. The gift of God's grace abounded, through Christ, to many. God's condemnation came as the result of one man's sin: God's justification covered many transgressions. The curse brought by one man is removed, and the blessing brought by one Man, Christ, takes its place.

The way of acceptance is the way of grace. Sin has reigned virtually supreme. It must give way to the grace of the Lord Jesus Christ, who in the life of the Christian ushers in a new reign which brings the believer to everlasting life.

> *Grace first contrived a way*
> *To save rebellious man;*
> *And all the steps that grace display,*
> *Which drew the wondrous plan.*
>
> *Grace all the work shall crown,*
> *Through everlasting days;*
> *It lays in heaven the topmost stone,*
> *And well deserves the praise.*

Philip Doddridge

NOTES

The Spirit of Life

IN this portion the apostle Paul introduces us to the work of the Holy Spirit in the Christian. Notice how often the words 'life', 'live', etc., occur, and how frequently they are associated with the Spirit.

Freedom through the Spirit (vv.1-8)
The glorious statement of verse 1 is a cause of great rejoicing to every Christian. The sentence of God's holy law, which every man has broken, binds us and pronounces death upon us. The gospel, which is the law of the Spirit of life, has delivered us from this imprisonment. What the Spirit does in our receiving the gospel is to declare that the Lord Jesus Christ has fulfilled the law and the requirements of God, and has also borne its penalty for us. Hence we are free. In Charles Wesley's famous words,

> *No condemnation now I dread;*
> *Jesus, and all in Him, is mine!*
>
> Charles Wesley

Submission to the Spirit (vv.9-11)
All men are under control. Unbelievers are under the control of their natures (although they mistakenly think that they control their natures). Because their natures are sinful, nothing they do pleases God, because they do not submit to God. Christians, however, are free, as we have seen. But they are free to do the will of God. This is true of every Christian, since every Christian has the Spirit of Christ and is controlled by that Spirit. This same Spirit, who brought life to our spirits, will one day bring life to our dead bodies.

Witness of the Spirit (vv.12-17)

Christians have a duty to perform, which is exactly the opposite of their previous compulsion to obey their sinful natures. They do not have life because they fulfil their obligations; rather they fulfil their obligations because they have life. Now that they have learned submission to the Spirit, they will enjoy one of the greatest privileges held out to the sons and daughters of God—being led by His Spirit. They are no longer slaves of sin and fear, but true children of God. Above all, they know they are Christ's because the Spirit assures their spirits that they are so. It is true that you may know that you are a Christian from certain evidences in your new life, but here Paul says that the Holy Spirit will tell you plainly that you are a Christian. The evidences may be examined and tested: the direct witness of the Spirit is above such examination.

NOTES

Christian Assurance

YOU will sometimes hear people speak of the Christian hope. The hope of the Christian is not something vague and uncertain, that may or may not be realized. This hope is described in Hebrews 6:18 as 'an anchor for the soul, firm and secure'. The hope of the Christian is that Christ will bring him to heaven, and thus it looks to the future. But because it is *Christian* hope it is as fixed as something already accomplished.

Hope for the creation (vv. 18-27)
In Genesis 3:17,18 we are told that the creation suffered as a result of Adam's sin. The curse fell not only on man and his descendants but on the plant and animal kingdoms also. Danger and ugliness abound in the world because of that first sin. In the same way the salvation won by the Lord Jesus Christ will also affect the creation. *Now* there are great sufferings; but think of the glory that will be. *Now* the creation itself appears to groan under the weight of sin; but one day it will be set free from its burden. The creation shares in our deliverance as it has shared in our sorrow. Paul gives no details of this, and therefore we need to be careful, but see Psalm 96:11-13; Psalm 98:7-9; Isaiah 11:6-9.

As we await the fulfilment of this hope, we have the Spirit's help in the frail and faulty manner of our praying.

Hope for the Christian (vv. 28-39)
How refreshing it is, among all the changing uncertainties that surround us, to find the promises of God's Word giving confirmation. Are you puzzled and distressed by the strange ways in which God deals with you? He is working for your

good. The supreme good He has designed for you is that you should be glorified, that is, be made at last like the Lord Jesus Himself. This is what God intended for you from the beginning, and therefore this is what God will accomplish for you. So sure is this, that what is yet future is spoken of as though past — 'those he justified, he also *glorified*.'

Nothing can stand in our way, and nothing can halt the march of God's purpose. Do you fear that someone will accuse you and condemn you before God? But it is God who accepts you, and it is Christ who has died for you. Do you think that anything will come between you and Christ? Death is the great separator and divides us from everything and everyone whom we love. But not even that grim enemy will separate us from the love of God and His Son, our Saviour.

The great errand has been fulfilled; . . . with the now admitted presence of our Forerunner within the veil to plead the accomplishment of it, nothing is wanting to the confidence wherewith we may now leave our cause in His hand and look for the sure mercies of David.

Thomas Chalmers

NOTES

Saved Through Faith

LIKE all good men, Paul had a great affection for his country and his countrymen. The intensity of his feeling for them is clear from chapter 9:1-5. His desire for their salvation, however, does not blind him to the unhappy fact of their rejection of the gospel he preached. There are three particular features of the Israelites which may be admired, but which do not of themselves bring salvation. Many religious people today follow the same sad pattern.

Zeal not enough (vv.1-4)
The apostle himself can bear testimony to the earnestness of the Jews. They seemed to spare no effort, and to spend all their energies in pleasing God. All was in vain, however, since they failed to recognize that the only righteousness God accepts is not that which we think *we* can present to Him, but that which *Christ* offers to Him. Their zeal is worthless because they ignorantly assume that they can buy God's favour on account of that zeal.

Hearing not enough (vv.16-18)
Although men must hear the gospel in order to be saved by it, it does not follow that everyone who hears God's Word is saved. Herod heard John the Baptist gladly (Mark 6:20), but it did him no good. Hebrews 4:2 tells us that, to some, hearing the gospel was unprofitable. In verse 18 Paul quotes the psalmist to show that the creation itself declares the glory of God, but to no avail.

Understanding not enough (vv.19,20)
The answer to Paul's question here is evidently 'yes'. Moses speaks of people who have 'no understanding', implying that

133

the Israelites did have understanding. As a consequence of not understanding who God was, these other nations did not seek or ask for God. The Jews had the advantage of having the Old Testament writings to help them come to a knowledge of God, and yet it was lost upon them. Now if zeal, hearing and understanding will not bring a person to God, what will?

The importance of faith (vv.5-15)
Salvation comes by faith alone. Moses describes a righteousness that comes by law-keeping. But already in chapter 3 of this letter Paul has said that there is no hope in that direction. Salvation is a question of believing and confessing. This is true for all men, Jews and Gentiles. Both are alike condemned as sinners (Romans 3). Now both alike have the way of salvation declared to them, through the preaching of the gospel.

Finally, note the long-suffering of God. Is there a more haunting, heart-rending verse in the Bible than verse 21?

NOTES

Quotations

Quotations are taken from the following publications:

Richard Baxter, *The Reformed Pastor* (Banner of Truth Trust)

John Brown, *Hebrews* (Banner)

Samuel Chadwick, *The Way to Pentecost*

Thomas Chalmers, *Lectures on the Epistle of Paul the Apostle to the Romans*

Stephen Charnock, *The Existence and Attributes of God*

Robert Haldane, *The Epistle to the Romans*

William Hendriksen, *Gospel of John; Gospel of Luke* (Banner); and *More Than Conquerors* (Presbyterian and Reformed)

Matthew Henry's *Commentary* (Marshall, Morgan & Scott)

Jamieson, Fausset & Brown, *Commentary* (MMS)

D. M. Lloyd-Jones, *God's Way of Reconciliation; Life in the Spirit in Marriage, Home and Work; Atonement and Justification* (Banner); *Faith on Trial* (Inter-Varsity Press)

F. B. Meyer, *Tried by Fire*

J. A. Motyer, *The Tests of Faith* (IVP)

Leon Morris, *1 Corinthians* (Tyndale Commentary, IVP), and *The Cross in the New Testament* (Paternoster)

G. Campbell Morgan, *The Acts of the Apostles* (Pickering & Inglis)

George Philip, *For Such a Time As This* (Didasko Press)

James Philip, *By the Rivers of Babylon* (Didasko)

A. W. Pink, *Gleanings in Exodus; Gleanings in Joshua* (Moody Press)

J. C. Ryle, *Expository Thoughts on the Gospels* (James Clarke)

A. M. Stibbs, *New Bible Commentary* (IVP)

J. R. W. Stott, *The Epistles of John* (Tyndale Commentary, IVP)

C. H. Spurgeon, *The Treasury of David; Sermon in Heavenly Meanings*

A. W. Tozer, *Keys to the Deeper Life* (STL Distributors)

Thomas Watson, *The Saints' Spiritual Delight*

Geoffrey B. Wilson, *1 Corinthians* (Banner)

E. J. Young, *Genesis 3; The Book of Isaiah* (Eerdmans)

OTHER BOOKS BY PETER JEFFERY FROM THE EVANGELICAL PRESS OF WALES

I Will Never Become a Christian
 – addresses the arguments and excuses of the convinced unbeliever.

Seeking God
 – a clear explanation of the gospel, written for the earnest seeker after faith.

All Things New
 – a simple, straightforward explanation of basic aspects of the Christian life for someone who has just become a Christian.

Walk Worthy
 – a sequel to *All Things New*, presenting clear guidelines on issues with which the new Christian will have to grapple during the early years after conversion.

Stand Firm
 – a young Christian's guide to the armour of God.

Christian Handbook
 – a straightforward guide to the Bible, church history and Christian doctrine. It provides in one handy volume a wide range of information which would otherwise only be found in much larger and more expensive volumes.

These are available from your local Christian bookshop, or in case of difficulty, from the publishers (postage extra):

> Evangelical Press of Wales, Bryntirion, Bridgend,
> Mid Glamorgan CF31 4DX, Wales.